Tomiwa Owolade writes about social, cultural and literary issues for the *New Statesman*, *The Times*, the *Sunday Times*, the *Observer*, UnHerd and the *Evening Standard*. He has appeared on BBC Radio 4 and Times Radio discussing some of the ideas in this book. He won top prize at the RSL Giles St Aubyn Awards 2021.

THIS IS NOT AMERICA

WHY
BLACK
LIVES IN
BRITAIN
MATTER

TOMIWA
OWOLADE

Atlantic Books
London

First published in hardback in Great Britain in 2023
by Atlantic Books, an imprint of Atlantic Books Ltd.

10 9 8 7 6 5 4 3 2 1

A CIP catalogue record for this book is available
from the British Library.

Hardback ISBN: 978 1 83895 621 9
E-book ISBN: 978 1 83895 622 6

Atlantic Books
An imprint of Atlantic Books Ltd
Ormond House
26–27 Boswell Street
London
WC1N 3JZ

www.atlantic-books.co.uk

Printed and bound by CPI (UK) Ltd, Croydon CR0 4YY

To Dr Adenle of Biket Hospital,
Osogbo, Osun State

CONTENTS

INTRODUCTION:
THIS IS NOT AMERICA

I began to reflect more intensely than ever before on what it means to be black and British in the summer of 2020: this was the year that radically changed the conversation on race in Britain. One incident from that time stands out. An open-letter email, written by current students, accused the English department of my old university, University College London, of racism towards black people. I was astonished; I had witnessed no racism when I studied there the year before. But I swiftly discovered the letter wasn't simply about that university. Neither was it about Britain in general. It was about America.

The year of 2020 was extraordinary. The Covid-19 pandemic led to many lost lives and isolated us from our friends and family. It was the year of the US presidential election. We fought bitterly over 'cancel culture'. Brexit was done, or seemed to be, after four years of internecine political conflict; but the rancour of that debate still carried on into other issues. The letter by the university students was not in direct response to any of this. It was part of a wider response to the murder of a middle-aged black man named George Floyd in Minnesota by a police officer called Derek Chauvin. This atrocity was filmed and went viral around the world.

The students at my old university wanted to show they cared about black people. They demanded that the English faculty should hire more black staff and teach more texts by black authors. But something strange about this letter caught my attention. They used the term 'BIPOC' to describe black and ethnic-minority people in Britain. This acronym stands for 'black, indigenous and people of colour'. BIPOC would make perfect sense in America: the United States has oppressed its black, Asian, Hispanic and indigenous people for centuries. But campaigning against the victimization of the 'indigenous' people of Britain makes one sound more like a far-right agitator than a progressive activist. It is more Nick Griffin, former leader of the fascist British National Party, than Molly, twenty-two, Labour Party activist from University College London. What was this acronym doing in a letter written by students to highlight the racism of a British institution?

The letter confirmed the dominance of America's racial politics over the rest of the world. Every continent, including Antarctica, saw protests expressing solidarity with black Americans. The summer of 2020 was characterized for many of us by reading articles, essays, tweets, memes, images, private messages and public announcements that expressed dismay at racism. Actors, musicians, sports stars, politicians, third and fourth cousins and influencers took to social media to denounce the mistreatment of black people. Corporations advertised their commitment to greater racial diversity in their workplaces. Museums promised to decolonize their collections. British retailers such as Sainsbury's and ASOS made donations to anti-racist organizations.[1] Many football clubs in the English Premier League adopted 'taking the knee' before the start of every match. Many responses were also personal. Many white people asked after their black friends, expressed shame that they had hitherto been quiet about racial injustice and committed themselves to speaking out against any racism they encountered among their family and white friends. Floyd was not the first black person to die recently after an altercation with the police. And it's true that there were some protests in

2014 after the death of another black man: Michael Brown in Ferguson, Missouri. But in their scope and intensity, the reactions to the events of 2020 dwarfed anything that had gone before.[2]

This is not a bad thing in itself. Much of this comes from a benign place: solidarity is worthy of praise rather than scorn. From the Civil Rights Movement to the fight against apartheid in South Africa, from the Arab Spring to the recent uprising by Iranian women against sexist theocracy, solidarity has played a vital role in animating social-justice movements throughout the world. But solidarity should not come at the expense of the truth. Expressing moral indignation at the murder of George Floyd is one thing; invoking the term BIPOC to condemn a liberal university faculty in England is another. The former is a moral response to tragedy and injustice. The latter trivializes this tragedy and undermines the case for social justice. If we lose sight of who and what we are fighting for, what is the point of fighting? This is why the truth matters. The response to George Floyd's murder abdicated this responsibility: it looked at race in Britain through the perspective of America.

Why did the death of George Floyd trigger the response it did? I think there were three overlapping factors. The Covid lockdown probably played some role. We were cooped up inside, as a matter of law, to

4

prevent the spread of a mysterious new disease. This was uncharted territory for all of us; we probably needed some sort of collective release. Another factor was the growing role of social media in our political and personal lives. When something spreads through Twitter and Facebook, it can easily morph into reality. In fact, it *is* reality. The greatest factor, however, was that we live in the shadow of America's culture and politics. When something significant happens in America, it reverberates across the rest of the world, and many of us interpret what is specific to America as true of our own country. The students at my old university, isolated from human contact by the pandemic, stuck online, and incubated in American culture from birth, condemned the racism of a British institution by following the script of America.

* * *

America is the most influential country in the world. During the night of the 3 November 2020 US presidential election, Britain and the rest of the world were hooked. It seemed like the most consequential night of the year. Like countless others, I was transfixed by the drama. I went to sleep at 1 a.m. just as Florida was called for Donald Trump. I woke up six hours later at seven and immediately checked Twitter. I was delighted when it was announced, a few days later, that Trump had lost the election and Joe Biden had won; I even considered buying champagne and ordering in pizza. All for an election in a country 3,000 miles away. I'm sure even the colonies of the British Empire did not treat the 1945 British general election with this level of rapt attention.

Britain watches America and sees its own politics through an American prism. Whenever a scandal breaks out, we affix the term 'gate' at the end of it – Beergate and Partygate – as an echo of America's infamous Watergate. When an important decision on a contentious issue like abortion is made – such as *Roe v. Wade* being overturned in the summer of 2022 – many British women are so devastated by the decision that they feel as if it is an attack on their own rights. The Supreme Court leak made the front cover on both centre-left and centre-right British national papers: the *Guardian* and the *Telegraph*. Many of us mourned Ruth Bader Ginsburg's death like she was one of our own: a beloved elderly relative rather than a senior judge in a foreign country.

Many of Boris Johnson's enemies call him the British Trump. His supporters, meanwhile, claimed he had a personal mandate when there was pressure on him to resign in early July 2022 over his lying about lockdown parties. But we don't have a presidential system; we have a parliamentary democracy. As Fraser Nelson put it in the *Telegraph*: 'Boris Johnson failed because he tried to impose a presidential model on a parliamentary democracy.'[3] Many young right-wing men in Britain view American conservative leaders as more worthy of emulation than their British counterparts. As the writer Will Lloyd wrote in an essay for *UnHerd*: 'These young Tories are stripping the American Right for parts. They believe that until the British Right comes out fighting, it will keep losing the culture.' One young British man said to Lloyd that 'Once the [United] States are taken back, it will influence conservatives here. Then the Tories will stop being so shit.'[4] Americans also look at our politics through the prism of theirs. A *New York Times* article in May 2022, for instance, wrote about the Labour Party's plan to win back the 'Rust Belt' seats of England from the Tories – as if the American Midwest and the English North occupy the same landscape.[5] Even if we are genuinely uninterested in what goes on over there, we can't escape the force and influence of American culture. We share the internet with them. As the British writer Helen Lewis puts it, 'sharing the internet with America is like sharing a rhinoceros. It's huge, it's there, and whatever it's doing now, you sure as hell know about it.'[6]

I can name all of America's presidents from 1933 till today. I could not do the same for the prime ministers of Holland or Belgium over the same time period: two nations just across the English Channel. This might be an anglophone prejudice, but I doubt many people can name the past or current political leaders of Australia and Ireland without checking (New Zealand's former prime minister, Jacinda Ardern, is the exception – she is very popular).

When the England football team was facing America in the group stages of the 2022 World Cup, the England players took the knee – the gesture conceived in America to protest against police shooting unarmed black men – but the American players did not.[7] This is an apt symbol for the current relationship between the countries. They set the trend; we follow.

This is about power. America is at the top of the cultural and political tree. And its influence is not simply confined to Britain or other anglophone countries. It is global. When the mandarins of the Académie française – the institution that closely monitors the health of French language and culture – complain about anglicisms corrupting the French language, what they mean are Americanisms. After the Second World War, one article in the popular

French newspaper *Le Monde* declared that 'Coca-Cola is the Danzig of European Culture.'[8] The Nigerian novelist Chimamanda Ngozi Adichie told the *Guardian* in 2022 that she thinks 'Europe imports America's cultural battles.' She adds that 'in some ways, America sets the standard of what we should be talking about and caring about. Europe should also take responsibility. And say, "You know what? No, thank you."'[9] Even Russian president Vladimir Putin, who defines himself as opposed to what he views as the decadence of American civilization, is utterly obsessed with American culture wars. As the writer Aris Roussinos puts it: 'How much weaker and more pathetic does Putin seem for the growing fixation on American culture war issues that manifests in his speeches? Rather than being outside the system of America's cultural power, he has revealed himself as trapped here with the rest of us.'[10]

But we are all influenced not only by America's political power; many of us are also seduced by the grand American Story. The nation has a set of ideals characterized by renewal and transformation: Manifest Destiny, the American Frontier, the American Dream, the City upon a Hill. Thomas Paine, the Englishman who became one of the most eloquent defenders of the American Revolution, wrote in his book *Common Sense*: 'We have it in our power to begin the world over again. A situation, similar to the present, hath not happened since the days of Noah until now.'[11] A redemptive arc is integral to how America sees itself: it was under the yoke of colonialism, but it became the land of liberty; it had slavery, but it abolished it. We are intuitively fascinated by such narratives. They possess the satisfying structure found in classical myths. The struggles of life are not fixed; they can be overcome.

The unvarnished truth is that America is an old nation. It was founded on written ideals, but it has the oldest codified constitution in the world still in use. The average age of a constitution in the world since the 1780s, when America established its founding document, is only nineteen years. As the British political philosopher John Gray states: 'American institutions have changed less over the past centuries than those of practically any other country.'[12] The American historian Timothy Snyder, meanwhile, has said that 'America is an old nation, but we claim to be new. We are the mid-life crisis of nations.'[13] What makes America attractive to the rest of the world is that Americans have claimed their values to be universal: everyone should aspire to them. In 1941 Henry Luce, the influential publisher of *Time* magazine, wrote an essay entitled 'The American Century', in which he argued for the United States to be a political, social and cultural world leader. After the Second World War, this vision became a reality.[14]

Britain, exhausted and facing steep imperial decline, passed the leadership of the anglophone world to America after the end of the Second World War. At that time, America possessed two-thirds of the world's gold reserves. Its per-capita income was four times larger than the combined per-capita income of Great Britain, France, West Germany and Italy. It was a leading producer in steel, electronics and aeroplanes. It was also a leader in military technology; it had a monopoly on nuclear weapons.[15] Janan Ganesh, the *Financial Times* columnist, has written that 'there is a case for Harry Truman [the US president] in mid-1945 being the most powerful human being who has ever lived'.[16] China might be the most powerful country within the next few decades. As of today, though, America still remains supreme.

And because America is the most influential country in the world, it makes sense that its racial politics are exported to the rest of the world. As Alastair Bonnett argues in *Multiracism*: 'The Americanization of the language of racism' reflects the 'cultural power of the USA'.[17] He adds that 'global institutions, such as the World Bank and the UN, have disseminated US-models of racial categorization and racism'. Black

Americans are the most influential black people in the world. This is not because they are black. It is because they are American. The American story of race, in the decades after the Second World War, spoke powerfully to Britain's newly arrived black citizens. Most of them were black Caribbean. This meant that most of them were – like black Americans – the descendants of enslaved Africans taken to the New World. Many of them were also profoundly alienated by the racism they faced when they arrived in Britain. They thought they were British, and they were right to think so: they were subjects of the British Crown. But they were made to feel like strangers. It's no surprise they looked to America. It was a country with a larger and more established black population. The British Black Panther was based on the counterpart in America. Malcolm X and Martin Luther King and Muhammad Ali were heroes to many black British people; they had so few heroes in their own country. America possessed a strong and sophisticated network of civil-rights organizations, from the NAACP (National Association for the Advancement of Colored People) to the SNCC (Student Nonviolent Coordinating Committee) and CORE (Congress of Racial Equality), which campaigned against gross injustices with a forthright moral conviction. They offered clarity. But black

Britons also looked to America for a more prosaic reason: British people from all backgrounds looked to America. (Richard Hoggart's 1957 book *The Uses of Literacy* laments the poisonous effects of American-led mass culture on the working-class communities of England after the Second World War.)

It is understandable why we in Britain are fascinated by America: we share a common language; the founding fathers of America were British subjects; many of Britain's greatest actors and musicians and directors made their name and fame in America; we voraciously consume American culture – from *The Simpsons* to *The Sopranos*. This is not necessarily a bad thing. This book is not anti-American. I love many aspects of American culture: I love the films of Martin Scorsese and Richard Linklater, the music of Bessie Smith and Don Headley, the fiction of John Updike and Philip Roth, the poetry of Ella Wheeler Wilcox, the comedy of Larry David and the visual art of Roy Lichtenstein. I love American food, from turkey stuffings to American candy. I love New York City and Los Angeles. And I also love many people in America – including my brother, who has lived in the country for nearly twenty years and now has an American wife. This account is also not anti-American in another sense. Many of the thinkers on race that I have been most inspired

13

by while writing it have been American, such as Ralph Ellison and James Baldwin. The arguments in this book are a vindication of these thinkers, who affirmed the importance of American citizenship to struggles against racism and rejected the view that you could reduce a person to their race. These are the arguments of *This is Not America*, but in a British context.

I am also not uncritically pro-British. There are parts of British culture I don't like or am indifferent to – in particular the weather, some of the food, the class divisions and some of the twee attitudes towards the royal family. In fact, being piously pro-British strikes me as fundamentally un-British; taking the piss out of ourselves is one of our greatest virtues. This book is not about being pro one nation and anti another. It is about accepting a nation on its own terms rather than through the perspective of another nation. Out of this, we can build a more effective form of anti-racist politics.

* * *

Britain is different from America. The United Kingdom of Great Britain and Northern Ireland is a constitutional monarchy and a parliamentary democracy. The United States of America is a federal republic with a presidential system. America, as mentioned above, has a written and codified constitution – Britain's constitution is unwritten and malleable. Britain's population is around seventy million people; America has more than 330 million residents. America is a richer country than Britain, and far more violent: the murder rate in Britain is 1.2 per 100,000 people, but in America it is over five times higher, at 6.3. In America, possessing guns in your home is legal under the constitution. In the UK, gun ownership is severely restricted, and we don't have a culture that valorizes the use of firearms.[18] As the *Times* columnist Hugo Rifkind points out, 'Gun-wise, particularly, only about ten Londoners get shot dead every year.' By contrast, in 'Washington DC, which is more than ten times smaller, the figure is 23 times more'.[19] America is also more punitive on crime. The incarceration rate for people in England and Wales is 131.5 per 100,000 people, rising to 134 for Scotland. In America, it is 716.

Abortion has been legally available up to twenty-four weeks in Britain since the 1967 Abortion Act (apart from in Northern Ireland, which only decriminalized abortion in 2019). Abortion varies state by state in America: in some states, like New York and California, a woman can legally get an abortion up to foetal viability; in other states, like Louisiana and Oklahoma, abortion is completely illegal.[20] At a federal level, abortion was decriminalized in 1973 with the Supreme Court decision of *Roe v. Wade*, which was reinforced in 1992 with *Planned Parenthood v. Casey*, and which established that women have the right to abortion up to the point when a foetus can live outside the mother. Both decisions were overturned, as I mentioned earlier, by the Supreme Court decision of *Dobbs v. Jackson* in 2022. Women in America have no national statutory maternity leave, and there is no universal healthcare in the country. In the UK we have the National Health Service. Male homosexuality stopped being a crime in the UK under the 1967 Sexual Offences Act. Many American states – especially in the South – didn't make gay sex legal until 2003. Britain is different from America in terms of political and legal institutions, population size, economy, crime, various axes of culture and values, and geography. It is a very different country.

This seems like an obvious point to make, but over recent years we in Britain have followed American politics and culture to such an extent that this important distinction has been lost. The Spanish-American philosopher and poet George Santayana once analysed the relationship between Britain and America, and the pitfalls that come with viewing one nation through the lens of another: 'The groundwork of the two societies is so similar,' he wrote, 'that each nation, feeling almost at home with the other, and almost able to understand its speech, may instinctively resent what hinders it from being at home altogether.' The fact that we have some affinities, in terms of language and culture, seduces us into thinking we can intuitively understand each other. 'Each will judge the other by his own standards,' Santayana added, 'not feeling, as in the presence of complete foreigners, that he must make an effort of imagination and put himself in another man's shoes.'[21] But making such an effort is crucial. Without making this effort, the important differences between each country – in terms of politics, culture and the demographic make-up – are obscured.

Santayana was writing in the first half of the twentieth century. As of today, however, the relationship between the two nations is closer to a phenomenon called 'cultural cringe', notably used by the Australian art critic Robert Hughes to describe the relationship between Britain and Australia. I think the concept also works well for Britain's attitude to America: 'the Cultural Cringe is the assumption that whatever you do in the field of writing, painting, sculpture, architecture, film, dance, or theatre,' Hughes wrote, 'is of unknown value until it is judged by people outside your own society.' He added that 'it is the reflex of the kid with low self-esteem hoping that his work will please the implacable father, but secretly despairing that it can. The essence of cultural colonialism is that you demand of yourself that your work measure up to standards that cannot be shared or debated where you live.'[22] Britain's relationship with America is a case of cultural cringe. All too often, we judge ourselves by America's standards rather than our own. Important differences between each country are lost amidst this.

One such important difference between Britain and America is race, and this will form the focus of this book. Over the past decade, racial topics have become much more visible in the British media landscape. As the researcher David Rozado puts it, in a blog post that was published in August 2022, 'over the last decade, various studies have suggested that the UK is now rapidly following the United States into a more polarized politics in which intensifying "culture wars" over issues such as racism, identity, diversity, the legacy of history, and "social justice" or so-called "woke" politics are becoming far more prominent'. Rozado adds that 'between 2010 and 2020, terms such as racism and white supremacy in popular UK media outlets increased on average by 769% and 2,827% respectively'.[23] The problem is that, all too often, these discussions reflect an American perspective.

Britain is not America: black British people are distinct from black Americans in many relevant ways. Black British people, for example, are overwhelmingly immigrants or the children of immigrants. The average black American, by contrast, can trace his or her ancestry in America further back than the average white American. The black British population only reached 1 per cent of the general British population for the first time in around 1980. Black people now constitute 4 per cent of the British population.[24] Since America's founding, however, the black American population has been between 12 and 19 per cent of the general American population. For a long while, black British people largely meant black Caribbean people. This is no longer the case. Over the past thirty years there has been a significant shift in the nature of the black British population: there are now twice as many black Africans in the country as black Caribbean people. Most black Americans are still the descendants of the enslaved Africans imported to America between the seventeenth and nineteenth centuries.

Race is different between the two countries in another sense, too: the racial composition of Britain and America. White people constitute 60 per cent of the population in America: in Britain, by contrast, they make up 81.7 per cent of the population. There are more than three times as many Asian people in Britain as black people: Asians now make up 9.3 per cent of the British population. In America, by contrast, there are twice as many black Americans as Asian-Americans. America also has a distinct ethnic group that numbers almost 20 per cent of the population – the Hispanic or Latino – for which there is no equivalent in Britain. In all of the above respects, race in Britain is different from race in America. This should come as no surprise: Britain's political institutions, history and many of its cultural values are different from those in America, so why should we assume that race would be the same between the two countries?

Many of us forgot these differences after the murder of George Floyd. On 25 May 2022 the British Labour Party announced that it would introduce a new Race Equality Act. As part of the announcement, the party released a video on social media explaining why Britain needed legislation to combat systemic racism. David Lammy, the Labour MP for Tottenham, was the first person to appear in the video. Near the start, he said this: 'George Floyd looked like me. He could have been me.'[25] But Floyd only looked like Lammy in the most superficial sense, and his life experience could only have been like Lammy's in the most superficial sense, too: in that they were both black. David Lammy is a British politician and lawyer representing a London constituency: he is not similar to George Floyd. George Perry Floyd Jr – known simply as Perry to his family and friends – was born in October 1973 in Fayetteville, North Carolina, to George Floyd Sr and Cissy Floyd. He was arrested more than twenty times in his life by the police, often for dealing drugs, and he spent almost one-third of his adult life in jail.[26] He also attended a segregated school, an experience that doesn't correspond to the experiences of black British people.

Ultimately the announcement was pointless. We already have the 2010 Equality Act, which supersedes the 1976 Race Relations Act and explicitly prohibits racist discrimination. It is not clear to me what a new Act would do. In the video Lammy adds that 'We face the issues of structural racism in our lives every day. That's why George Floyd's death sparked a global movement, stretching from Minneapolis to Manchester to Mile End.' Why should we assume that being a black person in Minneapolis is the same as being a black person in Mile End, apart from the magical powers of alliteration? Lammy doesn't enlighten us.

Racism is not the same everywhere in the world. Racism reflects norms, and norms are not universal. They depend on the social, cultural, economic and demographic background of a country. The racism against African migrant workers in Italy is not the same as the racism against indigenous communities in Australia; the discrimination against Indian labourers in Qatar is not the same as the genocide against Uighur Muslims by the Chinese Communist Party. There are some similarities between the racism experienced by black people in Britain and America because both countries have some cultural affinities, but there are also many important differences. They are different countries.

Historically, racial segregation has been a more prominent feature of American society than of British. Frederick Douglass was one of the greatest black Americans of the nineteenth century; he campaigned against slavery in America with extraordinary eloquence and vigour; he was one of the most photographed American men of his century. Throughout his life he compared Britain favourably to America. In a letter to his friend Amy Post, for instance, Douglass wrote this about his experience of visiting Britain: 'Everything is so different here from what I have been accustomed to in the United States. No insults to encounter, no prejudice to encounter, but all is smooth. I am treated as a man and equal brother.' He added that 'My color instead of being a barrier to social equality is not thought of as such. I am everywhere treated with the greatest kindness by all with whom I come in contact. The change is wonderful.' In another letter, to the influential American abolitionist William Lloyd Garrison, Douglass noted: 'I find no difficulty here in obtaining admission into any place of worship, instruction, or amusement, on equal terms with people as white as any I ever saw in the United States.'[27]

More recently, despite the discrimination in housing, employment, criminal justice and education that many black people faced in Britain after the Second World War, there was no equivalent in British law of the Jim Crow segregation (between the late nineteenth century and the mid-1960s) that was enshrined in America. Lynching has never been practised in the United Kingdom. Interracial marriage has never been banned in Britain. Our schools are not segregated by race, but by class. When the 1948 British Nationality Act was introduced, David Maxwell Fyfe, a barrister and politician for the Conservative Party, announced, 'We are proud that we impose no colour bar restrictions' and 'we must maintain our great metropolitan tradition of hospitality to everyone from every part of our empire'.[28] Famously, during the Second World War, many black American soldiers stationed in Britain were treated more kindly by white British people than they were by fellow white American soldiers. One West Country farmer was quoted in the *New Statesman* as saying, 'I love the Americans, but I don't like those white ones they've brought with them.'

In a 1943 column for *Tribune*, George Orwell wrote about walking through London during the Second World War: 'Even if you steer clear of Piccadilly with its seething swarms of drunks and whores,' he wrote, 'it is difficult to go anywhere in London without having the feeling that Britain is now Occupied Territory. The general consensus of opinion seems to be that the only American soldiers with decent manners are the Negroes.'[29] That year also witnessed the Battle of Bamber Bridge, where an attempt by the American military leadership to racially segregate the pubs in a Lancashire village was resisted by both the black American soldiers stationed there and the white British natives. The British-American journalist Christopher Hitchens recounts in his memoir *Hitch-22* his experience of talking to black American cab drivers who served in the Second World War. They had fond memories of England. As Hitchens put it, 'for many of these brave gentlemen, segregated in their US Army units,

England was the first picture they ever saw of how a non-segregated society might look'. He added that, 'in my hometown of Portsmouth there was a riot in 1943, with the locals scorning attempts by American military policemen to enforce a color bar in the pubs. The young Medgar Evers [a black American civil-rights activist] apparently told his English friends that after what he'd seen and learned, when he got back to Mississippi he wasn't going to put up with any more of this garbage.'[30]

This is not to say that racism has never played a part in the experiences of black people in Britain. Such a suggestion would be silly. It is merely to note the difference from America. The racism that black people subsequently encountered in the UK after the Second World War was much closer in nature to the racial hostility encountered by other immigrant groups. Like South Asians and other immigrant communities, they were treated as a drain on resources and a threat to national cohesion.

Even today, the differences between black Americans and black Britons on race are significant. It is much more normal for black Americans to have an exclusively black social circle than it is for black Britons. In December 2022 I attended my older brother's wedding in Nigeria. He was marrying an African-American woman (by which I mean a descendant of enslaved Africans, not an African immigrant or from an African immigrant family). She and my brother invited seventy guests to Nigeria, made up of family and friends, and every single one of them was black. It is easier to have exclusively black friends in America than it is in the UK because there are so many American cities where the majority of the population is black: from Memphis, Tennessee, to New Orleans, Louisiana; from Newark, New Jersey, to Baltimore, Maryland; from Birmingham, Alabama, to Detroit, Michigan. And there are many more examples. (According to the latest census data, Atlanta, Georgia, is only 49 per cent black.) By contrast, London is the city in Britain with the highest concentration of black people and they only make up 13 per cent of the city's population.[31] Any comparison between black people in America and black people in Britain, without considering these demographic differences, is short-sighted. When we think about race and racism, we need to think about the groups that are affected by these things. They are not simply interchangeable pegs to be slotted into a machine. They are human beings richly embedded in their own particular communities. Emphasizing that humanity needs to form a key part in any anti-racist vision.

Another problem with invoking the experience of black Americans to describe black British people in the way Lammy did in that video is that it defines black people simply in terms of victimization. Despite the racism that many black British people have faced in Britain, the *Windrush* generation and subsequent generations of black British people have developed a strong cultural affinity with the nation. To define them *wholly* through their terrible experiences is a form of denigration: it denies their attachment and contribution to Britain. Some of this affinity is explicit: for instance, through sport and music and religion. The former footballer Ian Wright is as inextricably British, for example, as any white person from south London. Some of this affinity, meanwhile, is implicit, through cultural assumptions and behaviour: the unwritten norms, such as our ability to form a queue seamlessly, that make us British. All of it is negated by seeing black British people through the lens of America, and only as victims of racial oppression.

Black British people are not one single group. We are the largely Christian *Windrush* generation and its direct descendants. But we are also the Muslim Somali refugees who arrived in the 1990s and 2000s. We are affluent and well-educated immigrants from Nigeria and Ghana who arrived at around the same time as the Somali refugees and now live in Kent and Hertfordshire, and send their kids to private and grammar schools. And we are the Congolese immigrants in inner-city London who send their kids to the local comp. We are Kemi Badenoch and Bernardine Evaristo, two highly successful women with Nigerian ancestry, but with different experiences, occupations and political beliefs. Badenoch is a Tory politician who is touted as a future leader of her party. Evaristo is a Booker Prize-winning novelist and president of the Royal Society of Literature. We are barely a *we*. To quote the famous line from the American poet Walt Whitman: we 'contain multitudes'.[32]

English is the unifying language. But we often speak or listen to a language other than English at home. Anyone who takes a bus ride across south-east London – through Peckham, Lewisham, Woolwich and Thamesmead, what I like to call the black African Riviera – will hear Yoruba, Twi, Somali and African-accented French: the language of immigrants from francophone Africa. The parents of a close friend of mine come from Cameroon. His dad is from the minority English-speaking part of the nation; his mum comes from the 80 per cent of the country that speaks French. My friend speaks English, like any other young Londoner. Black Britons have also intermarried with native white British people, especially the working-class and Celtic white population, at a remarkable rate. As Trevor Phillips, a *Times* columnist and former chairman of the Equality and Human Rights Commission, has said, Britain is one of the few countries in the world with a large mixed-race population that came about as a result of love rather than rape.

Still, our current conception of black British identity is limited. When that friend of mine asked a white university-educated woman, 'Where do you think my family is from?', the only two places she could name were Nigeria or Ghana. I'm fairly sure that she could name most of the southern states of America. This reflects a wider problem. Think of the most famous black people in the world, and the chances are most of the names that crop up in your mind will be black Americans. In fact think of the most famous black people in history and you get a similar result. I'm not using this to judge. I am as guilty of this as anyone else: Martin Luther King, Rosa Parks, Toni Morrison, Oprah Winfrey, Nina Simone, Will Smith, Barack Obama, Muhammad Ali, Michael Jackson, Michael Jordan – their names ring around my mind like a child reciting the players of his favourite football team. American cultural frames can be all-consuming.

This book argues two main points. We should understand race in Britain through a British perspective, and we shouldn't reduce black people to their race. Being black and British is as much shaped by being British as it is by being black. The only way to approach racism in Britain helpfully, and to acknowledge the distinctive qualities of black people in the UK, is by accepting this particular duality: black *and* British. Race is not an abstract or metaphysical thing. It relies on context – national context, in the case of distinguishing the experiences of black British people from black Americans, but other forms of context, too. For instance, when we talk about black British people, we have to recognize that we are not talking about a singular group of people: we are talking about different communities and cultures, divided by language and religion and national origin and class. When we focus on race in Britain, therefore, we need to take into account the unique complexities of black British identity. Despite such differences, however, there are also striking similarities between the communities that fall under the category of black British – an emerging dialect called Multicultural London English (MLE), for example, which is now used by younger black British people of all backgrounds and even, increasingly, by younger British people of all backgrounds, irrespective of their race or where they live in the country. The experience of black British people is not only defined by racism, and it would be profoundly damaging to suggest so: it has also been characterized by love and tenderness and humour and friendship. It has been an incorrigibly British experience.

This is Not America is not a history book about black British people. Nor is it a definitive account of contemporary black Britain, or of race relations in Britain today: events are moving so rapidly that an exposition of that ambition will only be impressionistic in any case. As I mentioned earlier, up until the past twenty years the majority of black British people came from a Caribbean background, and this is no longer the case: today most black British people are black Africans. In terms of history books about black British lives, I would recommend Hakim Adi's *African and Caribbean People in Britain*; David Olusoga's *Black and British*; *Windrush* by Trevor Phillips and Mike Phillips; and Peter Fryer's *Staying Power*. In terms of titles on immigration to Britain, I would recommend *Bloody Foreigners* by Robert Winder and *Lovers and Strangers* by Clair Wills.

One might argue that one problem with this book is that it replicates the problem of seeing race in Britain through an American perspective, by focusing on the experiences of black people in Britain despite the fact there are more Asians in the country. This is a fair criticism. But I can only write about what interests me, and I am interested principally in black people in Britain. I welcome any account that rejects the American frame by focusing on the particular experiences of British-Asians. Another related objection to the book is this: by writing an entire title on the topic of race, am I not already acquiescing to an American way of looking at the world? I would respond by saying that ignoring the issue will not make it go away. But what if it is the case that Britain has internalized so much of American culture that it is useful to simply accept this trend as a matter of fact and look at black British people through an American perspective? I would say the underlying differences between the countries still matter, and should still be taken into account when looking at race. Another objection one might make is that I put too much store in evidence and facts, and this fog of data diminishes the experiences of black British people. To which I would respond that the truth matters, and empirical evidence is important. But I accept that this can only go so far. This account will not be solely data-driven, but will try to capture what data can't encapsulate by itself: the substance of human experiences. The point is that to accept the humanity of black people, or anyone else, you can't define them as a homogenous bloc; the differences within and between them matter just as much. This is why I will strive for *experiences* rather than the singular experience.

Perhaps the most pressing concern about a book with this argument is that I undermine the case for cross-national solidarity, and that I deny or underplay the existence of racism. On the point of solidarity, as I mentioned earlier in this chapter, I think it's a noble thing. But I don't think it is the only thing that matters. It should be balanced by a respect for the truth: concern or interest in the race relations of one country should not distort understanding of race in our own country. On the question of denying or underplaying racism, I do the opposite: I take it more seriously than the people who think racism explains every inequality in our society, or those who believe racism defines every aspect of black people's lives. The former position is a distortion of reality, and the latter is a distortion of the humanity of black people. Anti-racism must be based on a respect for reality and the humanity of black people.

This latter point is a personal one for me. Whenever I write about race in columns and essays, some people object to it by claiming that I deny the existence of racism. Some of this objection takes the form of nasty insults. I am accused of being a coon, a house Negro, an Uncle Tom, a kapo. Still, many of my intellectual heroes – such as James Baldwin,

Ralph Ellison, Bayard Rustin, Zora Neale Hurston – were often denounced in these terms during their lifetimes.[33] I think it's a sad indictment of the nature of race conversations that anyone who deviates from the orthodoxy is criticized in this way. Which makes me all the more passionate to keep pushing against this orthodoxy.

We need a new conversation on race in Britain. This is the aim of this book. What is at stake here is the dignity of black people in Britain. We need to stop seeing them through the lens of American racial politics or through an abstract lens that emphasizes their blackness over their Britishness. The damage that will be done by seeing black Britons through the perspective of black Americans, or through an abstract black identity, is that it stops us from precisely identifying the racial inequalities in our society – the issues that face them and other ethnic-minority people in the country. It also undermines another case for anti-racism. Racists think black people cannot be British; that they are black before they are British. They are wrong. But the reason why they are wrong is because we accept that black British people are British. This should be central to any form of anti-racist politics. Without it, we cede to the racist argument that black people are inescapably foreign to Britain.

This is Not America is a polemic with interconnected observations and arguments: black British people are not black Americans; black British people are not all the same, but they nevertheless constitute a distinct group on the basis of their shared British identity; many black British people in the past and today look to America as a template for understanding themselves; but in order to understand a group of black people – including black Americans – you need to understand them on their own terms. The same is true of black British people, which means, for instance, that understanding the history of immigration is crucial to understanding the forms of racism that black British people have experienced, and the positive and negative relationship they have with Britain today. Comprehending the history of colonialism is also crucial, but it should be approached with a clear commitment to accuracy over revisionism, and good faith over tribalism.

The problem with many of the most prominent race activists and political figures in Britain today is that they do not approach race with this sufficient level of sensitivity to the facts. Instead they treat the subject in a simplistic and patronizing way. One of the reasons this is a problem is because race is a slippery concept, and we need to be more nuanced in how we approach it: terms like BAME (black,

Asian and minority ethnic) have limited use, and the experiences of 'mixed-race' people around the world illustrate the importance of national and cultural context in making sense of racial identity. Ultimately, it is only by accepting the fact that black British people are already integrated into British society that we can build an effective form of anti-racist politics, one that is both humane and grounded in reality. This is not America; black British lives matter.

Part 1

THIS IS AMERICA

1

DOUBLE CONSCIOUSNESS

Black and British: two equally important identities. But we can understand why racial solidarity exists, is seductive even, and why many black people emphasize their racial identity over and above other forms of attachment that might define them – such as their attachment to a place. They do this as a shield against racism. Racial solidarity is a form of belonging, when other forms of belonging are denied to you – such as your sense of belonging to a nation. If you are denied the same rights as your fellow citizens on the basis of your race, or you are treated as a foreigner in any other way, then it makes sense to opt for an identity that crosses national boundaries. And to attach yourself to people who share your racial identity and are marginalized in their own country.

Blackness thus becomes a substitute for Britishness.

Black *and* British can thus seem as if they are in tension, because black people have sometimes been made to feel like they do not belong in Britain, and so have leaned into their racial identity as an alternative source of belonging. But the most convincing case against racism is not to fall into the trap of embracing your racial identity above all else. It is to show that there is more to you than your racial identity. There is your religion, your family, your home city, your individual experiences. There is also your nation. Racists think someone's race is the only important thing about them. Anti-racists should reject this. Focusing only on their race undermines somebody's humanity; it denies the variety of their lived experiences. You can't humanely approach black British people by focusing only on their blackness.

The same is true of black Americans. The *American* matters just as much as the *black*. The United States, though, has historically denied the political, legal and social rights of its black population. Black people in America have often been made to feel more black than American. Against this racist imposition is the fact of their American identity. W. E. B. Du Bois hypothesized this tension – between black and American – and gave a name to it: double consciousness. This chapter looks at the concept of double consciousness, and argues that it comes from an American context. The struggle to reconcile blackness and Americanness, and the argument that those things are in fierce tension, are coming from an American frame of reference.

In the first chapter of his acclaimed essay collection, *The Souls of Black Folk*, Du Bois writes: 'One ever feels his two-ness, – an American, a Negro; two souls, two thoughts, two unreconciled strivings; two warring ideals in one dark body, whose dogged strength alone keeps it from being torn asunder.'[1] Understanding the 'two souls' of black Americans is crucial to understanding their identity. For Du Bois, these souls are in conflict with each other. They are unreconciled. And it is easy to see why he believed this: he lived between 1868 and 1963. He was born five years after the Emancipation Proclamation Act that abolished slavery in America, and he died the year before the Civil Rights Act that abolished segregation.

Du Bois was one of the greatest American intellectuals of the twentieth century. He was also, in the words of his biographer David Levering Lewis, 'the premier architect of the civil rights movement in the United States'.[2] His death was announced on the day of one of the most important events in the American Civil Rights Movement: the 1963 March on Washington. Just before Martin Luther King gave his iconic 'I Have a Dream' speech, Roy Wilkins, then head of the NAACP, stepped up to the podium to announce that Du Bois, who was one of the founders of the NAACP, had died. The culmination of the long struggle for civil rights came the day its intellectual lodestar died in a foreign country – in Ghana, 3,000 miles away.

After Du Bois's death, condolences came from all over the world: Nikita Khrushchev of Russia, Jomo Kenyatta of Kenya, Ahmed Ben Bella of Algeria, Walter Ulbricht of East Germany, Kim Il-Sung of North Korea. Mao Zedong and Zhou Enlai also expressed sadness at his passing – Du Bois's birthday soon became a national holiday in communist China. No one from the American embassy in Ghana was there at his funeral. By this time, Du Bois had renounced his American citizenship and had embraced an ideology and movement that spanned the world: communism. He had formally joined the Communist Party three years previously, in October 1960, when almost everyone else had left because of the ruthless crushing of the 1956 Hungarian revolution. Du Bois was a proud anachronism: by the time he died, at the age of ninety-five, he was more radical than when he was twenty-five. He was eventually buried in Osu Castle in Ghana, where

European slave traders had captured many Africans and taken them from there to the New World. He had, in one sense, come home. But Du Bois was an American – not an African. And despite his later affinity with an internationalist ideology, much of his earlier and most influential work was dedicated to questions of nationhood and race. What it meant to be a black American.

Du Bois was also an uncommon type of black American. He was born and brought up in New England, in the town of Great Barrington, at a time when most black people in America came from the Deep South. He had French Huguenot ancestry, but insisted that his name should be pronounced in the Anglo-Saxon style as 'Due-Boyss' rather than the Gallic 'Doo-Bwah'. After studying at Great Barrington High School, he took a bachelor's degree at Fisk University, the historically black college in Tennessee. This was his first taste of the American South. But fourteen out of the fifteen faculty members of Fisk were white, abolitionist, northern and overwhelmingly Congregationalist; the very same people Du Bois was accustomed to from his childhood. It was a liberal arts college. Students were taught Greek, Latin, French, German, theology, history, natural sciences and moral philosophy. The purpose of the university was to create an African-

American version of the New England elite. Du Bois later took another bachelor's degree and obtained a PhD at Harvard: in doing so, he became the first black American to be awarded a doctorate at Harvard University.

He was a black man who funnelled himself through the institutions reserved for a white American elite. For Du Bois, 'the history of the American Negro is the history of this strife': the strife between the Negro and the white American. He said that the American Negro 'would not Africanize America, for America has too much to teach the world and Africa', and 'he would not bleach his Negro soul in a flood of white Americanism, for he knows that Negro blood has a message for the world. He simply wishes to make it possible for a man to be both a Negro and an American.'[3] He sought to explain why the hard division between Negro and American was false. He himself was living proof of that.

* * *

I have never really suffered from double consciousness. Much of my frustration with contemporary anti-racism is the conviction that I am more than being black. But I am often seen for my race and little else. Because black people have historically been victimized by white people, this means I am seen as a victim in need of rescue. I chafe against this. This is not an intellectual response from me; I feel at a gut level this kind of 'activism' or 'allyship' is patronizing. But there is also a robust logical case against it. If you don't treat black people with the same moral standard as white people, you exclude them from the circle of humanity. I have felt this strongly for a very long time – before I started to look seriously into the subject of race. It was not always the arguments that were made in defence of this worldview that triggered a negative response from me. It was the tone. A mixture of pity and sanctimony. Two incidents from my late teens illustrate my frustrations.

The first dates from when I was applying for university. One of my teachers, a sweet and eccentric Scottish woman called Ms Stuart (not her real name), suggested I apply to SOAS, a university apparently famed for its generosity towards black and ethnic-minority students. Her intentions were noble. She wanted to give me a helping hand in terms of my university opportunities. Maybe I should have been grateful. But my immediate response to her suggestion was a visceral mixture of offence and embarrassment. This was offensive to both SOAS and me. The university is more than a charity for black kids, and I was more than the sum of my race. I smiled at her and acknowledged her advice. But later that evening I removed SOAS from the list of the universities I would apply to. It was tainted indelibly by her condescension.

I had a feeling that Ms Stuart's primary motive was to show me that she was a good person. It wasn't a matter of sincerity; I'm sure she genuinely believed she was doing good. And I still think of her as a good person and have no ill-feeling towards her. Her suggestion was aimed at improving my life. The problem I had with it was the idea that my whole person could be reduced to my race. Her display of benevolence came at the expense of my humanity. I didn't just want to be *the black guy in university*. I knew I was much more than that.

I was sensitive to being patronized by my teacher or by any other white person in authority because I was inculcated with pride by my parents. Not a racial pride, though I and my family are not ashamed to be black, but one of character. And I think part of the reason why I don't have double consciousness is (paradoxically) because I am an immigrant. This is a paradox because you would think my added 'foreignness' would be a hurdle to navigate. But I did not come to the UK because my forebears were stripped of their home, language and culture and were trafficked to a foreign land where they were traded, brutalized, raped and marked as inferior (which describes black Americans and black Caribbean people). I arrived instead as an immigrant from an independent African country. At home we often spoke Yoruba, the language of my ancestors. I don't have an English name. Yet I don't feel a conflict or a tension between blackness and Britishness, because I don't feel my black identity is something I need to defend or hold onto; I am completely at ease with it. I have not been cut off from my roots. Double consciousness thus makes sense in America precisely because many black Americans have had their blackness demonized and marginalized by white American society. But it doesn't apply to me because I have a different set of experiences.

My experience is not universal. Other black British people have had experiences more closely resembling that of Du Bois – the desperate search to marry blackness and Britishness. An example is the novelist Caryl Phillips. Like Du Bois, his ancestors were enslaved Africans. He was born on the small Caribbean island of Saint Kitts in 1958 and moved to Britain when he was just four months old. He grew up in Leeds and attended Leeds Central High School, an all-boys grammar school. His family was the only black family in the council estate where he lived. Phillips and his brothers were also the only black pupils in the school he attended. This relative isolation continued when he started studying English at Oxford.[4]

There were only two black African students in his Oxford college. And neither of them felt any personal connection to Britain: 'their affair with Britain,' Phillips writes in his essay collection *Colour Me English*, 'was conducted on the understanding that they had a home to which they could return. I envied them.'[5] Phillips, in their sense, didn't have a home to return to; he was inescapably English. He had no recollection of Saint Kitts. All his childhood memories were shadowed by the landscape of Leeds. He was a Yorkshire boy. Although England was his home, he felt he never truly fitted in. He was often made to feel like an outsider.

Then Phillips met another black person at Oxford. His name was Emile Leroi Wilson, and he was a black American. Wilson was an ambassador for 1970s black American culture: he possessed a 'broad afro', 'half-mast checkered flares' and 'gold-rimmed pebble glasses'. He was handsome and charismatic. And he introduced terms like *jive-ass, hip, cat, dude* and *funky* to a demure and short-sighted lad more used to demotic Yorkshire slang. At first there was a big cultural mismatch: Emile 'had nearly as much trouble understanding me as I had trying to understand him'. But they eventually became friends and, in Emile, Phillips ultimately found a way out of his racial isolation.

Phillips was envious of Emile's sense of a black identity. He writes that his black American friend 'seemed more confident, to have a cogent, if somewhat aggressive, idea of who he was and, as he would put it, where he was coming from'. Because of this, 'I found myself exhilarated by his company, but also panicking inside because I was so much less sure of myself.' Emile's confidence exposed Phillips's lack of it. Emile's knowledge of who he was, the traditions to which he belonged, emphasized Phillips's racial insecurities. Emile would not only be an ambassador for black America; he would also encourage Phillips to connect with black people in the UK. To do that, Phillips would need to go to a city fifty miles away from Oxford to, as he put it, '"plug into" black life'.[6] That city, of course, was London.

London provided Phillips with a richer source of identity than Leeds or Oxford. He could finally spend time with a large group of black people – drinking, chatting, taking pleasure in a shared set of experiences. He was soon leading a double life. By day he was an English student in one of the most revered and ancient universities in the world; by night he was a reveller in a brand-new black British urban scene. He would leave

Oxford during the evenings to visit Ladbroke Grove and Brixton. While in the capital city, he would drink in rowdy pubs and visit exciting nightclubs. If he ever missed the last train back to Oxford from Paddington station, he would take the tube to Heathrow airport and sleep in the Terminal 3 lounge. Then he would wake up at dawn and get back to Oxford to attend an early-morning lecture on Early Modern lyric poetry. It was an exciting life – he had finally developed a connection with black communities, while still maintaining his attachment to Oxford. But it was also exhausting, and it would finally break Phillips. You can't be Dr Jekyll and Mr Hyde for ever.

At university he was interested in drama and wanted to be a film director. He directed the plays of Shakespeare, Tennessee Williams, Harold Pinter and Henrik Ibsen for student productions. But Phillips soon had a nervous breakdown: he was drained by academic work, theatre work and trips to London. So he took time off university, and finally took up Emile's offer of visiting America. He was leaving the country that his parents thought was the motherland, to visit the motherland of the friend who introduced him to black culture. Phillips went on an all-American road trip.

In his travels through America, he encountered casual racism as deeply chiselled into the social landscape of the United States as the faces of its presidents on Mount Rushmore. In an Alabama hotel lobby, for instance, a woman referred to him as 'boy' and expected him to carry her bags up to her room – she didn't stop to consider whether or not he worked in the hotel; she even offered to tip him one dollar. In Salt Lake City he was waiting in a queue to pay for a carton of orange juice, but the man at the till ignored his turn and instead served the white woman behind him. Phillips was indignant, but this was impotent fury; he knew he couldn't individually change this widespread culture of degradation.

A week later, when he was in a small town thirty miles south of Los Angeles, he discovered two novels that would change his life: *Invisible Man* by Ralph Ellison and *Native Son* by Richard Wright. Reading *Native Son*, in particular, made him want to be a writer. Phillips found transcendent works of beauty in these two fictional titles that concerned the racial politics of America. In the case of Ellison's *Invisible Man*, what struck Phillips was the sense of an individual being made invisible not because of a magic trick or superstition: it was because no one wanted to see him. Phillips also developed a great love for the work of James Baldwin.

Caryl Phillips is now a distinguished novelist, essayist and a professor of English at Yale University.

He won the James Tait Black Memorial Prize for Fiction in 1993 for his novel *Crossing the River*, and the Commonwealth Writers' Prize in 2004 for *A Distant Shore*. America was where Phillips found his ambitions first reflected back at him. 'It was in the United States,' he writes, 'that I made the "discovery" that it was possible for a black person to become, and sustain a career as, a writer.'[7] America – as it is for so many people who visit the country – was a nation of self-transformation. Growing up in the Britain of the 1960s and 1970s, Phillips was not shown what it was like to be someone he wanted to be: 'In British schools I was never offered a text that had been penned by a black person, or that concerned the lives of black people.' In a sense, it was in America that he first felt visible; it was where he first felt seen. His racial identity was treated, for the most part, as something worthy of pride rather than scorn or callous indifference. Through his encounter with his American friend, Emile, Phillips recognized that most black people were not Oxford-educated boys from Yorkshire. And some black people had a surer sense of themselves; this was the sort of black person Phillips wanted to be. And America provided a powerful template for this. He struggled to find a way of attaching himself to a rigid British identity, so he found it in a wider black identity that was influenced by American culture.

Phillips first came to America about a decade after Du Bois's death. In the 1960s, meanwhile, the challenge to reconcile a black identity with an American identity continued among the generation that followed in the footsteps of Martin Luther King, the leading civil-rights activist in America. James Meredith was one of them. He tried to racially integrate the University of Mississippi. On 5 June 1966 he began a one-man march: the Meredith March Against Fear. He did this so that he could exercise his right, as an American citizen, to walk through the whole of Mississippi, one of the most viciously racist states in America, without intimidation or harassment. On the second day of the march he was shot and wounded.

Another follower of King called Stokely Carmichael carried on the march from 7 to 26 June. Carmichael, at that time, was a member of the SNCC, an organization of young activists closely aligned with King's Southern Christian Leadership Conference. But he soon developed a reputation as a radical hero in the tradition of Malcolm X. As Peniel E. Joseph, Carmichael's biographer, puts it, since Malcolm was dead, 'Carmichael now took his place alongside Martin Luther King as one of America's two most important black political leaders.'[8]

On 17 June 1966 King told Carmichael to stop using the phrase 'Black Power'. Carmichael refused. This marked the start of the Black Power phase of the Civil Rights Movement. In the summer of that year American president Lyndon B. Johnson privately predicted that Carmichael would be killed in three months. He would live for another thirty years. In 1967 he went on a five-month world tour.

Like Du Bois, Carmichael was an internationalist. He believed America was so hostile to its black population that black people needed to have a more cosmopolitan outlook; they needed to break free from their attachment to America. There is a fundamentally antagonistic relationship between the identities 'Black' and 'American'. Likewise, black people in other Western nations needed to break from any sort of attachment to these oppressive states. They needed to look to the Global South. For Carmichael, 'Black Power means that black people see themselves a part of a new force, sometimes called the Third World; that we see our struggle as closely related to liberation struggles around the world.'[9] From Algeria to Vietnam, and from Angola to Mozambique, oppressed communities, according to Carmichael, were dominated by Western forces. Joining up with the Third World, Carmichael declared, was the 'only salvation' for black people in America because 'we are fighting to save our humanity. We are indeed fighting to save the humanity of the world, which the West has failed miserably to preserve. And the fight must be waged from the Third World.' He added with great confidence: 'There will be new speakers. They will be Che, they will be Mao, they will be Fanon. You can have Rousseau, you can have Marx, you can even have the great libertarian John Stuart Mill.' It was the West versus the Rest. And Carmichael was on the side of the Rest. In this reasoning, blackness (or simply being non-Western) could represent the belonging that is needed against the marginalization of racism.

Pan-Africanism is a branch of internationalist anti-colonialism that Carmichael espoused. It is the worldview that the interests of black people in one country are shared by black people around the world. The Organization of African Unity, which was founded in 1963, defined Pan-Africanism as 'an ideology and movement that encouraged the solidarity of Africans worldwide. It is based on the belief that unity is vital to economic, social and political progress and aims to "unify and uplift" people of African descent. The ideology asserts that the fates of all African peoples and countries are intertwined.'[10] It added that 'at its core, Pan-Africanism is a belief that African peoples, both on the continent and in the diaspora, share not merely a common history, but a common destiny.'

But Pan-Africanism was not created by black people in Africa. It was created by black people in the West. According to Hakim Adi, Britain's foremost historian of Pan-African thought, there are two strands of Pan-Africanism: 'The earlier form emerging during the period of trans-Atlantic enslavement,' he writes, 'originated from the African diaspora, stressed the unity of all Africans and looked towards their liberation and that of the African continent.' The second strand, however, 'emerged in the context of the anti-colonial struggle on the African continent in the period after 1945. This form of Pan-Africanism stressed the unity, liberation and advancement of the states of the African continent, although often recognizing the importance of the diaspora and its inclusion.'[11] These strands are interlinked. The second strand derived its ideas from the first: many of the leaders of newly independent African nations were not only inspired by older generations of black people in the diaspora; the leaders in both strands were educated in the West.

Pan-Africanism is a Western ideology, which assumes that you can understand the struggles of a black man in Alabama through the prism of a black man in Abuja. But the progressive doctrine that a group of people share a destiny would be strange to many of the native religions and customs of Africa, where the cyclical nature of human existence is affirmed and the cultural differences between tribes are acknowledged as an enduring fact rather than a superficial imposition. Pan-Africanism asserts that there is an arc in history for black people that bends towards greater justice. This is a Western prejudice.

The same is true of Third World internationalism. It is also a Western ideology. Carmichael, as he said, adored Che Guevara, Mao Zedong and the political philosopher Frantz Fanon. And he compared all of them in opposition to Mill and Rousseau and Marx. But the radical thinkers Carmichael venerated espoused ideas that first emerged in Europe rather than the Third World: Marxism, in the case of Che and Mao; and universalist anti-colonialism, in the case of Fanon. Carmichael was a child of the West; his attempt to escape Western ideas was itself Western in character.

Kwame Nkrumah was also educated in the West and inspired by radical Western ideas. He was one of the leading voices against colonialism in the middle of the twentieth century and was the first leader of an independent Ghana, which was the first black African nation to gain independence from a European colonial power. Nkrumah is an icon of Pan-African thought. In 1963 he was a founding member of the Organization of African Unity. In that same year he also published a book entitled *Africa Must Unite*. But Nkrumah's higher education was conducted in America and Britain. He gained degrees in sociology, economics and philosophy at Lincoln University and the University of Pennsylvania. In Britain he studied anthropology at the London School of Economics, philosophy at University College London and law at Gray's Inn court. He was also busily befriending British communists and anti-colonial activists in Bloomsbury, and debating politics in cheap cafés in Camden. Nkrumah was baptised a Catholic and once considered becoming a Jesuit priest. He famously danced with Queen Elizabeth II when she visited Ghana. And he visited her again when she was at her summer residence at Balmoral, where a picture was taken that Nkrumah considered one of his most favoured possessions till the day he died.[12]

Another radical anti-colonial leader who was profoundly attached to the West was Léopold Sédar Senghor. In 1960 he became the first president of an independent Senegal. In the 1930s he was a pioneer of the intellectual movement Négritude, which asserted that a distinctive spirit unites black people across the world. Throughout his life he emphasized the importance of African unity. But it's striking just how Westernized he was. Senghor was educated at the Sorbonne, one of the elite institutions of higher education in France, and passed the highly competitive *agrégation* exams, while coming from a colony where most of the population was illiterate. He was later a teacher at French universities and an acclaimed poet in the French language. He was a Catholic from a colony where more than 90 per cent of the population was Muslim. Négritude was not conceived in the villages or towns of Senegal, or any other African territory, but in the city of Paris, along with émigré black intellectuals such as Aimé Césaire of Martinique and Léon Damas of French Guiana. Senghor was the first black person to be admitted to the extremely selective Académie française. After his long stint as president of Senegal, he died in a scenic town in Normandy, where he was living with his wife. She was white.[13]

The first Pan-African conference, moreover, was not held in an African country. It was held in London in 1900. And it was not organized by an African, but a Trinidadian man named Henry Sylvester Williams. The Pan-African Congresses were held in Paris, London, New York and Manchester before they finally reached an African city – Dar es Salaam in 1974. Marcus Garvey, one of the heroes of the Pan-African movement, and consecrated by the Pan-

African Rastafarian movement, never visited Africa in his life.[14]

Carmichael, like Du Bois, died in Africa. They both thought the fight for justice was the fight for 'the humanity of the world'. They believed it must be conducted from the Third World against the First World: America and Western Europe. But even as they disavowed their American identity, they betrayed it. They were not just Western in how they saw the world; they were especially American. The language of salvation – saving a corrupt world and transforming it into something perfect – has shaped America's ideological and religious movements throughout its history. Stokely Carmichael, the sixties black radical, often sounded a lot like the seventeenth-century governor of the Massachusetts Bay Colony, John Winthrop, who invoked the notion of a 'City upon a Hill' to redeem humanity from damnation.[15] When you strip to the core what Carmichael and Winthrop said, they both expressed a quintessentially American notion that a group of people can rescue humanity from its degraded position. For Carmichael, it was blacks and the other oppressed minorities of the world. Despite his avowal of an African identity, Carmichael's statements illustrate how intensely American he was. The reality is that the black American population, of which he was a member, is different from the black communities across the world to which he tried to demonstrate a rock-strong affinity. It's different because Americans are different, and black Americans are Americans.

Du Bois is recognized as one of the founders of Pan-Africanism. The idea that one could unite black people around the world thus emerged from someone grappling with an American problem: how to unite black people in his own country with America. Caryl Phillips sought inspiration for his black identity, moreover, not in Africa but in America. Magnificent writers like James Baldwin and Ralph Ellison provided the model for how a writer should be. Phillips's best friend at university was the black American Emile, not the African students.

But both Baldwin and Ellison were writers who started from a better premise than Du Bois, and had a greater level of self-awareness than Carmichael. For them, blackness and Americanness were not 'warring ideals'. They took it for granted that they were American. And they didn't look to the Third World for inspiration; they accepted that they were part of the West.

Caryl Phillips sought universal inspiration in a culture that is particular. He looked at his black identity through the frame of America – a country foreign to him – rather than through his own country.

When Ellison's unnamed protagonist in *Invisible Man* claimed he was not visible, he didn't mean his blackness was marginalized. He meant his humanity. All the other forms of attachment he had were cut off from him. One of them was the link between his blackness and his Americanness. The lesson we ought to learn from this is that black Americans constitute a distinct group of people who face a particular set of circumstances, shaped by the history and culture of America. They are not a symbol for black people across the rest of the world. They are black *and* American. They should be understood on their own terms.

2

AMERICAN INTEGRATIONISM

Ralph Ellison was the greatest exponent of American integrationism: 'Negroes,' he wrote, 'have been Americans since before there was a United States.'[1] For him, it was simply a matter of fact that black people are integral to America. The renowned black American intellectual Cornel West has argued that 'it's impossible to be a serious student of American culture and Afro-American culture without working through Ellison. He's the brook of fire through which one must pass.' The American academic Farah Jasmine Griffin, meanwhile, has said: 'If you read Ellison, there are two things you know. Number one: he loves black people. Number two: he loves the United States of America.'[2] For Ellison, these two things were not 'warring ideals'.

They were twinned. There is no America without black Americans.

To help us understand that Britain is not America, we should first see America as a distinctive country rather than as a model to interpret race in other countries. American integrationism is the idea that black people are integrated into American society. You can't understand black American culture in isolation; you can only understand it as congruent with American culture. This is not simply true of mainstream black culture and ideas; it is also true of the radical ideas that reject America. The thinkers and activists who espouse these ideas reject America in an American way, and I will explore this more fully in the next chapter. Once this is established, we can better appreciate how racial identity is informed by national context in other countries, too – including Britain. And from there, we can build a better understanding of what it means to be black and British.

Ellison stood out like a beautiful peacock: he used to wear grey tweed jackets, exquisite hats and two-tone shoes. His moustache was always perfectly trimmed. He was born in Oklahoma in 1914 – which was a frontier state that only became part of America in 1907 – and rose to the summit of mid-twentieth-century literary America with grace and flair.[3] But Ellison grew up in grinding poverty. His dad died when he was three, and his mum was a domestic worker. His father, a construction foreman, wanted him to be a poet. His mother tried everything she could to cultivate his intellectual and aesthetic interests – she used to bring back home discarded books, magazines, titbits and music recordings. Ellison was nourished on scraps. Nevertheless, he did more than survive this relatively impoverished upbringing. He thrived. He soon became a gifted musician; he was a trumpeter in his high-school band. And he subsequently won a music scholarship to attend the most famous black higher-education school in the American South: the Tuskegee Institute. This was the former home of the black American leader Booker T. Washington, the most famous black man in America in the first decade of the twentieth century, a hero to Malcolm X and a visitor to the White House. Music was Ellison's abiding passion, and this was how he got into the institution, but literature was what he became known for in his lifetime. And it is what he is known for now.

His first and only completed novel, *Invisible Man*, came out in 1952 and established him as the pre-eminent black American novelist of his generation. Many consider it to be the greatest American novel of the twentieth century. The book won the National Book Award for fiction; Ellison was the first black author to win this. He was also later awarded the Presidential Medal of Freedom, was made a Chevalier of the Ordre des Arts et des Lettres and given membership of the American Academy of Arts and Letters. All of this was for his immense contribution to literature and criticism. But his success back then, and today, rests almost entirely on that single and singular book.

Invisible Man is a novel, as the title suggests, about not being recognized. The first page contains this striking sentence: 'I am invisible, understand, simply because people refuse to see me.'[4] Ellison's unnamed narrator and protagonist is 'invisible' because his experiences are not viewed on their own terms. They are viewed through a narrow ideological perspective. White progressive liberals simply see him as a victim who needs to be rescued. Black nationalists only see him as a vehicle for righteous indignation against racism. Both of these groups are different, but they share one thing in common: they only see him for his race and nothing else. His individual experiences and attachments – what makes him a human person – go unrecognized. By not giving his protagonist a name, Ellison illustrates how even something he takes for granted, his own name, is not mentioned by those around him. He is a blank canvas upon which others can paint their assumptions.

'They were very much the same,' the narrator writes about progressives and black nationalists, 'each attempting to force his picture of reality upon me and neither giving a hoot in hell for how things looked to me. I was simply a material, a natural resource to be used.' This leads the narrator into existential despair. He is screaming at them: look at me for who I am. But they are only recognizing one part of his character. They are not seeing the full picture. This angst is captured in one especially devastating paragraph in the novel:

> *I was never more hated than when I tried to be honest. Or when, even as just now I've tried to articulate exactly what I felt to be the truth. No one was satisfied – not even I. On the other hand, I've never been more loved and appreciated than when I tried to 'justify' and affirm someone's mistaken beliefs; or when I've tried to give my friends the incorrect, absurd answers they wished to hear. In my presence they could talk and agree with themselves, the world was nailed down, and they loved it. They received a feeling of security. But here was the rub: Too often, in order to justify them, I had to take myself by the throat and choke myself until my eyes*

bulged and my tongue hung out and wagged like the door of an empty house in a high wind.[5]

Ellison's narrator is strangled by the expectation that he must conform to other people's expectation of how he, a black person, must behave. But what shaped Ellison's own aesthetic vision was not a sense of shame at being black: it was the opposite. Ellison is proud of his black identity. He merely thinks this has been diluted by a rigid dogma. He wants to reclaim this identity, but on very specific terms – as something consistent with his American identity rather than in opposition to it.

He not only believed black Americans are American. He also believed America is in large part black. In his essay 'What America Would Be Like Without Blacks', published by *Time* magazine in 1970, he argued with great eloquence that 'if we can resist for a moment the temptation to view everything having to do with Negro Americans in terms of their racially imposed status, we become aware of the fact that for all the harsh reality of the social and economic injustices visited upon them, these injustices have failed to keep Negroes clear of the cultural main-stream; Negro Americans are, in fact, one of its major tributaries.' Ellison especially highlights the importance of language in black Americans influencing the American mainstream:

> *And whether it is admitted or not, much of the sound of that language is derived from the timbre of the African voice and the listening habits of the African ear. So there is a de'z and do'z of slave speech sounding beneath our most polished Harvard accents, and if there is such a thing as a Yale accent, there is a Negro wail in it – doubtless introduced there by Old Yalie John C. Calhoun, who probably got it from his mammy.*[6]

Looking back at the history of popular American culture and up until the present day, it is undeniable that black people have made an extraordinary impact on American identity. It is impossible to conceive of America without incorporating its black citizens: Louis Armstrong, Denzel Washington, Muhammad Ali, Nina Simone, Richard Pryor, Toni Morrison and a galaxy of other cultural luminaries. On the relationship between black people and America, Ellison further added that 'Materially, psychologically and culturally, part of the nation's heritage is Negro American, and whatever it becomes will be shaped in part by the Negro's presence. Which is fortunate, for today it is the black American who puts pressure upon the nation to live up to its ideals.'

The language of putting 'pressure upon the nation to live up to its ideals' recalls the moral stature of another influential black American writer: James Baldwin. Baldwin was similar to Ellison. He was a great black writer *and* a great American writer. You can't understand the former without understanding the latter. Throughout his career, even as he condemned American racism in the most emphatic terms, Baldwin did so as someone who consciously saw himself as an American – someone who invoked the ideals of America. He was on the cover of *Time* magazine in May 1963 – on the 100th anniversary of the Emancipation Proclamation that liberated enslaved black Americans.

In a 1974 televised conversation between Baldwin and Maya Angelou, the poet and memoirist, they briefly stop to ponder the question of national identity. 'I believe we are Americans,' Angelou says tentatively. 'You believe it?' Baldwin queries sharply, 'I know it.'[7] He spent large chunks of his adult life in continental Europe and, at the time of their conversation, lived in an exquisite house in Saint-Paul de Vence in the south of France. Baldwin was even awarded the *Légion d'honneur* (the highest French order of merit) by President Mitterrand in

1986. But he was always an American: 'We've paid for this country,' he tells Angelou. 'That's why I can never leave it. You can't leave home, you carry it with you.' Elsewhere he writes that a black American is 'as American as the Americans who despise him, the Americans who fear him, the Americans who love him'.

Like many people, Baldwin only recognized how American he was when he was living in a foreign land. As his biographer, James Campbell, put it: 'He acknowledged a large debt to Europe, but the most important thing Europe could give him was his own identity. That identity was not European, nor was it African, nor was it even principally Negro – it was American.'[8] Baldwin had moved to France to liberate himself. As his mentor Richard Wright once said to an interviewer in *Ebony* magazine in 1953, 'Every Negro in America carries all through his life the burden of race consciousness like a corpse on his back. I shed that corpse when I stepped off the train in Paris.' Working as a writer in Paris in the decade after the Second World War, Baldwin realized he was just as American as any 'Texas GI. And I found my experience was shared by every American writer I knew in Paris.' That white Americans had their origins in Europe, and black Americans had their origins in Africa, was irrelevant: white Americans 'were no more at home in Europe than I was'. By contrast, he felt alienated from black people in Paris who were not Americans. He said to Harold Isaacs, 'Whenever I was with an African we would both be uneasy… the terms of our life were so different, we almost needed a dictionary to talk.' Baldwin, who raged against the racial injustice of America with searing eloquence, and who spent the last years of his life in an eighteenth-century mansion in rural France, was always bound to the country of his birth: America.

* * *

This sense of being bound to one's homeland is true more widely of the many Americans who have fought for equality and justice on issues of race and gender and class in the twentieth century. The historian and author Michael Kazin published an essay in 2002 for *Dissent* magazine in which he emphasized the patriotic element of many American social-justice movements: 'For American leftists,' Kazin writes, 'patriotism was indispensable. It made their dissent and rebellion intelligible to their fellow citizens – and located them within the national narrative, fighting to shape a common future.'[9] For instance, Elizabeth Cady Stanton, the nineteenth-century American feminist, invoked the Fourteenth Amendment that guarantees equality to all citizens of America, to push for equality for American women. She made her 'Woman's Declaration of Rights' on the centennial date of America's Declaration of Independence.

Kazin uses other examples. He writes that when the political activist Eugene Debs 'became a socialist, he described his new vision in the American idiom, as "the equal rights of all to manage and control" society'. Frederick Douglass, meanwhile, never ceased to cling to the ideals of the American Republic: 'After emancipation, Douglass never stopped condemning the hypocrisy of white Americans – or continuing to base his hopes for equality on traditions he and they held in common.'[10] The Americanness of these movements and individuals is not simply a matter of ideological or historical affinity. It is a matter of fact. They are not Americans simply because they want to be. They are American because they are.

In a 1993 interview between the TV broadcaster Charlie Rose and the cultural critic Stanley Crouch, the latter confidently asserted that 'Anybody who's an American who thinks that he or she is more of an Italian or more of an African, all they need to do is go back to that place that they think they're more from and they'll find out that they're Americans.'[11] In another interview between the two men, five years later and on the same show, Crouch revisited this theme. He claimed that if you flew Patrick Buchanan, the conservative thinker who has passionately railed against large-scale immigration, and Louis Farrakhan, the leader of the Nation of Islam, on a plane from America to Dublin, they would bicker ferociously all the way. But when they arrived in Dublin, the Irish would say: 'ahh, two Americans'. And if you flew them to Accra in Ghana, the Ghanaians would also say: 'ahh, two Americans'. Crouch concluded from this that there's something 'that hooks us all up that everybody recognizes except us'. Another example demonstrates this observation. In one episode of the American HBO show *The Sopranos*, Tony Soprano and his mob visit Italy.[12] One of his colleagues, Paulie Gualtieri, is delighted by the prospect of visiting the motherland for the first time. But as he travels through the country, trying to make conversation in his halting Italian and his Jersey-accented English, Paulie comes across as a complete stranger to the native Italians. The viewer soon realizes something stark: despite the gestures they make towards Italian food and phrases, these mobsters are indisputably American.

But what is the something that makes an American an American? Richard Wright, the first black American novelist to be a bestselling author in the twentieth century, gave some idea of it when he wrote in his 1941 book *12 Million Black Voices* that 'we black folk, our history and our present being, are a mirror of all the manifold experiences of America. What we want, what we represent, what we endure is what America is. If we black folks perish, America will perish.' Wright adds, crucially, that 'The differences between black folk and white folk are not blood or color, and the ties that bind us are deeper than those that separate us.' Ultimately, 'the common road of hope which we all travelled has brought us into a stronger kinship than any words, laws, or legal claims'.[13] In other words, it is a shared history that unites the different racial communities who live in America.

Another thinker who shared Ellison's perspective on the connection between blackness and America was one of his closest friends: Albert Murray. He first saw the distinctive name of Ralph Waldo Ellison on a Tuskegee library card in 1935 (Ellison's father named him after the nineteenth-century writer Ralph Waldo Emerson). Murray, at that time, was nineteen, three years younger than Ellison, and he had recently arrived at Tuskegee from a little hamlet in rural Alabama called Magazine Point, where his father was a labourer and his mother was a housewife. They were not, however, his biological parents. His birth parents were middle-class folk in a neighbouring town who gave him up to avoid a social scandal.[14]

Murray was a tall, slender and dark-skinned black man with a long face, reminiscent of a portrait by Van Dyck. He was a great talker: he could speak with great eloquence about Count Basie, Thomas Mann, William Faulkner, the twentieth-century British anthropologist Lord Raglan, and American ragtime music. But much of his energy and erudition was dedicated to melding his black identity with his American identity. Like Ellison, he was as American as apple pie.

Murray and Ellison went to the same school, but their friendship bloomed a few years later in New York. They first met in 1942 and began a great conversation, in person or through correspondence, that emphasized their cultural attachment to America. Murray's provocative collection of essays, *The Omni-Americans*, resembles Ellison's *Invisible Man*. Published in 1970, *The Omni-Americans* argues that America is neither a white nor a black country. It is, instead, 'incontestably mulatto'.[15] Black and white Americans share a culture, but racial difference obscures this fact. Murray was arguing this at a time – during the fag end of the civil-rights revolution – when distinct forms of black identity were increasingly prominent. Black Power was in vogue: men and women adorned themselves with massive Afros, dressed stylishly in bright dashikis and confidently intoned the slogan 'Black is Beautiful'. Many black Americans, like Stokely Carmichael, also felt an affinity with oppressed non-white groups around the world – from Algeria to Vietnam. But here was a middle-aged black man with a professorial face who said: you are Americans first and foremost, not Africans. As Murray writes, recalling the convictions of Stanley Crouch in Charlie Rose's show:

> *Identity is best defined in terms of culture, and the culture of the nation over which the Anglo-Saxon power elite exercises such exclusive political, economic, and social control is not all-white by any measurement ever devised. American culture, even in its most rigidly segregated precincts, is patently and irrevocably composite. It is, regardless of all the hysterical protestations of those who would have it otherwise, incontestably mulatto. Indeed, for all their traditional antagonisms and obvious differences, the so-called black and so-called white people of the United States resemble nobody else in the world so much as they resemble each other.*

A black kid in Mississippi resembles a white kid in Michigan more than he resembles a black kid in Mozambique. An old black lady in New York resembles an old white lady in North Carolina more than she resembles an old black lady in Nigeria. The cultural, linguistic and geographical similarities between black and white Americans override racial similarities between black Americans and black people in other parts of the world. This is Murray's contention. But what explains the tendency to deny the fact that black Americans resemble white Americans more than they resemble other black people around the world? Murray blames it on an approach to identity that fixates on abstract theory over specific realities. 'They encumber themselves,' he writes of many race theorists and activists, 'with those irrelevant theoretical and sometimes completely phony issues and highly questionable abstractions such as race pride, black identity, black consciousness, black art, black beauty, and the like, instead of striking directly at more concrete problems.' There is no such thing as a universal or essential black identity; these are meaningless abstractions. But there is a specific black American identity. Identities are mediated by context. They grow, snag, meld and transform under a particular rhythm, just like the jazz so beloved by Murray and Ellison.

Ellison, Baldwin and Murray's ideological descendants inherited their insistence on the affinity between black and white Americans. In an essay for *The Atlantic* magazine in May 1995 the writer Robert Boynton argued that, by the early 1990s, America had established a group of black intellectuals to rival the earlier generation of New York Intellectuals – the group of largely Jewish mid-century writers and essayists who wrote for publications like *Partisan Review*, *Commentary* and *The New York Review of Books*.[16] Some of the new black intellectuals, like Toni Morrison, wrote novels. Some of them, like Henry Louis Gates, occupied prestigious roles at universities: Gates was chair of Afro-American studies at Harvard University. Some, like Shelby Steele and Glenn Loury and Thomas Sowell, were conservatives, while others like Cornel West were on the radical left. These intellectuals wrote for magazines and newspapers, appeared on television programmes, wrote bestselling books and won prestigious prizes. They constituted a heterogeneous group in terms of their ideological outlook. But what united them was, as Boynton puts it, an aversion to rigid identity politics. They moved away 'from race-based identity politics to the importance of American citizenship for race relations. That is, they have thought less exclusively about the meaning of "blackness" and more inclusively about what it means to be an African-American – taking pains to scrutinize both sides of the hyphen.' In other words, they had assumed the mantle of integrationism.

The same was true of the New York Intellectuals. This earlier group was a galaxy of renowned novelists and critics: Philip Rahv, Lionel Trilling, Alfred Kazin, Irving Howe, Saul Bellow, Elizabeth Hardwick, Susan Sontag and Daniel Bell. Their work, 'Composed with the care of the expert and the passion of the anti-specialist,' Boynton writes, 'moved easily between literary and political judgments before bringing them together in a larger moral conclusion.' In particular, this group of writers was committed to art as something that transcends fixed categorization. But they still retained an American outlook. 'As intellectuals, they adopted a cosmopolitan style; as writers,' however, 'they sought a place in the tradition of American literature. Being Jewish didn't play much of a role in either pursuit.' As Irving Howe puts it: 'The New York intellectuals were the first group of Jewish writers to come out of the immigrant milieu who did not define themselves through a relationship, nostalgic or hostile, to memories of Jewishness.' Their grandparents or parents might have been immigrants from Eastern Europe, but these intellectuals were distinctly American. Alfred Kazin wrote fluently about American literature from Melville to Faulkner. They all loved Henry James. The opening lines of *The Adventures of Augie March* by Saul Bellow are: 'I am an American, Chicago born – Chicago, that somber city – and go at things as I have taught myself, free-style, and will make the record in my own way: first to knock, first admitted; sometimes an innocent knock, sometimes a not so innocent.'[17] Bellow was a Jewish-American integrationist.

Ellison was a close friend of Bellow, and he also wrote for a number of magazines associated with the New York intellectuals. He wrote that 'what the Jewish American writer had to learn before he could find his place was the American-ness of his experience'. He did this not by denying his Jewish roots and identity, but rather by filtering them through an American perspective: 'He had to see himself as American and project his Jewish experience as an experience unfolding within this pluralistic society.'[18] Ellison, and many subsequent black intellectuals, felt that black Americans needed to do the same. They thought you could affirm the visibility of a black American identity by acknowledging its relationship to a wider American identity. Ellison was an integrationist.

American racial integrationists believed that to be black and to be American were inextricably connected: one of the evils of racism was in denying this very connection. The most famous integrationist of the twentieth century was Martin Luther King. He believed America would not be able to realize its full potential unless she accepted that its black population was as fundamentally American as its white population. The problem with America is its failure to realize such ideals – not that these ideals are mistaken. In other words, integrationists situated their black identity within a larger American identity.

Black nationalists, by contrast, believe there is an irreconcilable tension between being black and being an American. They think such ideals of equality are fundamentally misguided because they can never be realized. Black people are not Americans; they are Africans trapped in America. Clinging to the dream of greater equality obscures the enduring and unavoidable reality of racism. In contrast to the optimism of people like Martin Luther King, black nationalists have a fatalistic attitude to race relations. They think racism will not be solved as long as black people rely on the goodwill of white people. Black people, instead, need to collectively organize around their own distinct identity.

The most famous American black nationalist of the twentieth century, at least until 1963, was

Malcolm X. He believed that trying to integrate public institutions like schools was a folly; he was sceptical about the Civil Rights Movement's insistence on passing legislation that banned segregation. He called the March on Washington – where King made his 'I Have a Dream' speech – the 'Farce on Washington'. Malcolm also claimed to be a 'victim of Americanism' and could see no 'American dream'. He could see only 'an American nightmare'.[19] In the 1964 American presidential election, when Lyndon B. Johnson faced Barry Goldwater, the Republican candidate who was against the federal government banning segregation, Malcolm X endorsed Goldwater. But this was more a rejection of the American mainstream than an affirmation of the American right. In 1964 Malcolm stated that 'I'm not a Democrat. I'm not a Republican, and I don't even consider myself an American.' He added that 'Those Honkies that just got off the boat, they're already Americans; Polacks are already Americans; the Italian refugees are already Americans. Everything that came out of Europe, every blue-eyed thing, is already an American. And as long as you and I have been over here, we aren't Americans yet.' Malcolm believed black people were a separate nation within America. 'Americanness' was a noose around their neck, choking every inch of dignity out of them.

Ellison acknowledged the heinous crimes against black people perpetrated by the American state: centuries of brutal slavery, followed by the terrorism and sadistic violence encouraged by Jim Crow legislation. The common slights and indignities on the street: being called a 'nigger', a 'Coon', and being refused access to public services and amenities by your compatriots. But he didn't allow himself to be defined by this. This brought him some criticism in his lifetime. Irving Howe was a public intellectual at *Dissent* magazine who criticized Ellison for not being politically engaged enough. According to Howe, *Invisible Man* was an insufficiently political book because, as a black man, Ellison had failed to properly face up to something that he should never have avoided: the pervasive fact of racial oppression. Ellison had this to say in response: 'One unfamiliar with what Howe stands for would get the impression that when he looks at a Negro he sees not a human being but an abstract embodiment of living hell.'[20] One of the reasons Ellison was proud of his black identity was because he viewed it as more than suffering. Black Americans certainly faced discrimination and terror and were thus often alienated in America, but they were fundamentally integrated into many parts of American culture – its language, its music, its literature and its sport. Capturing black Americans in the round thus meant not defining them solely in terms of their oppression. Ellison was critical of the black Americans who emphasized only the negative aspects of America and denied their attachment to the nation. For him, this was destructive:

> *Yet, like its twin, the illusion of secession, the fantasy of a benign amputation that would rid the country of black men to the benefit of a nation's health not only persists; today, in the form of neo-Garveyism, it fascinates black men no less than it once hypnotized whites. Both fantasies become operative whenever the nation grows weary of the struggle toward the ideal of American democratic equality. Both would use the black man as a scapegoat to achieve a national catharsis, and both would, by way of curing the patient, destroy him.*

Acknowledging the Americanness of a black American man is simply acknowledging his reality. This serves a vital purpose: it makes the black American *visible* rather than invisible. Ellison loved America not because he hated black people, but for the opposite reason: he loved America because he recognized that the nation to which he belonged was in a large part black, that it had already incorporated his identity as part of itself. His racial identity was not abstract or timeless; it reflected back to him his particular national context. This same is true of black people in other nations. It is particularly true, for instance, of Baldwin's adopted homeland: France.

* * *

Another way to think about how racial identity and the ideas associated with it are influenced by social context is by comparing them to language. Pierre Capretz looked like the archetypal Frenchman: he had luxuriant hair and his shirt was always buttoned very low, to form a sharp V on his chest. When speaking, even in perfect and nearly accentless English, he performed the ebullient hand gestures of a Gallic storyteller in a bistro or on a boulevard. He was born in Mazamet, a small town in the south of France, and died in Aix-en-Provence, a city near the French Riviera. But for more than fifty years of his life Capretz taught at Yale University. He taught the French language to American young people and the wider American public – and he was remarkably successful at it. 'If you look at what he created,' said Ruth Koizim, another professor of French at Yale, about his courses and programme, 'it still ranks among the best in terms of learning languages.'[21]

Capretz was not only an archetypal Frenchman. He was also a distinguished translator.

He was born in 1924 and moved to America in 1949. He first moved to Florida and initially taught Latin at the University of Florida. Soon he found his métier by teaching French instead. At first he discovered that his native language was taught using boring textbooks: students were encouraged to read books with French and English words side-by-side, and to learn French almost by rote; this method didn't work. Capretz had a better idea: 'I thought we had to change the way we were doing it,' he said, reflecting on his early years, 'and that a better way to teach French would be to put the students in front of what I call real French – that is, French that is used in real contexts.'[22] In other words, the best way to learn the language was by fully immersing oneself in it. When he moved to Yale in 1956, he started to develop his learning programme and called it 'French in Action'. It would revolutionize the learning of French in America.

He believed that, in order to learn a language adequately, you need to familiarize yourself with the contexts in which that language is used. Capretz used video, audio aids and took 10,000 photographs in France. He was bringing the sights, sounds and smell of French into a New England classroom.

The French language, he was convinced, couldn't properly be taught without creating a solid sense of the French world. In 1987, decades into the programme, a Boston-based broadcasting channel called WGBH, in collaboration with Yale and Wellesley College, turned 'French in Action' into a fifty-two episode television series. It became a romantic comedy featuring a beautiful young French couple. The protagonist was a young blonde student called Mireille. There were no English subtitles. And each episode was punctuated by mini-lessons led by Capretz, in which he would go over the scenes viewers had just watched, elucidating the nuances of the interactions between characters. In short, we would see and hear French in action.

For Capretz, meaning and context are inseparable. We know the meaning of a word because of how it is used. This is why the scenes don't use translations: 'French is not a translation of English,' he explained in the first episode of the series. 'It is not English that has been coded into French. No, French is French.' A French word exists on its own terms: 'when French people say something in French, it is not that they really mean it in English… when they say something in French, they mean something French.'

Salut, for instance, doesn't mean hello. *Salut* means *salut*. It can mean hello. But it can also mean goodbye. The meaning of *salut* is shaped by the context of its use; it is its own word, defined by a set of circumstances that are distinct from any English equivalent of the word. Language does not exist in a vacuum. It is a social activity, and social activities are not static but adapt to circumstances. We learn a language by practising it. This may seem patently obvious when it comes to language. But it's also true of race. Race is social, not abstract. We should look at race in a similar way to how we look at language. Both derive their meanings from context.

Language is also related to memory, and the associations of a language can evoke powerful associations that can't be translated into another language. They are so intimate. The British philosopher R. G. Collingwood, in his book *The Principles of Art*, expressed it like this: 'The English tongue will only express English emotions; to talk French you must adopt the emotions of a Frenchman. To be multilingual is to be a chameleon of the emotions.'[23] Emotions are the stock of experiences; to use a language is to inhabit a different emotional landscape, to occupy a somewhat different set of experiences. That most French of words, *baiser*, can mean both 'to kiss' and 'to fuck'.

Like Pierre Capretz, Frantz Fanon was a Frenchman. They were even born in the same year. Unlike Capretz, however, Fanon was black, and he was not born in mainland France, but in a colonial outpost of the nation: the Caribbean island of Martinique. Fanon became a global icon of black radical politics. He was claimed by both Algeria and America. The American Black Panther activist Eldridge Cleaver once said that 'every brother on a rooftop' could quote Fanon. Stokely Carmichael called him one of his 'patron saints'.[24] Fanon's classic 1961 book in defence of the Algerian War of Independence, *The Wretched of the Earth*, is a bible of anti-colonial politics. Near the end of it, however, Fanon writes this: 'All the elements of a solution to the great problems of humanity have, at different times, existed in European thought.'[25] Fanon identified with a tradition of thought that emerged from Europe and, in particular, France: the Enlightenment. As the *London Review of Books* writer Adam Shatz puts it in an essay on Fanon, 'he thought of himself as a son of the French Revolution rather than as an African, and the struggles in the colonies as a sequel to the storming of the Bastille'.[26] The first three words Fanon learned to spell were '*Je suis français.*'

He did not subscribe to the view that there is an essential black soul that distinguishes black people from white people. He was a universalist: he believed we all shared a common humanity. As he put it in his first book, *Black Skin, White Masks*, 'We shall demonstrate that what is called the black soul is a construction by white folk.' Instead, he tried to affirm the universal brotherhood of man: 'we must recall,' he writes, 'our aim is to enable better relations between Blacks and Whites'.[27] But Fanon was also self-aware enough to acknowledge that his belief in a common humanity came from a particular cultural perspective: 'As those of Antilleans, our observations and conclusions are valid only for the French Antilles – at least regarding the black man on his home territory.' This value of universalism was inculcated into him by his French lycée education. 'When you hear someone insulting the Jews,' one Martiniquan teacher informs him, 'pay attention; he is talking about you.' It is no surprise, then, that Fanon was sensitive to anti-Semitism: 'Anti-Semitism cuts me to the quick,' he writes. 'They are denying me the right to be a man. I cannot dissociate myself from the fate reserved for my brother.'

He was born to a bourgeois family in Martinique; his father was a civil servant and his mother was a successful shop owner. Martinique was an old colony, and many of its institutions were modelled on metropolitan France: schools, courts and hospitals. Fanon attended a fee-paying lycée, a privilege that neither poor West Indian blacks nor poor whites in mainland France could afford. He later fought for de Gaulle's Free France during the Second World War and was decorated with a Croix de Guerre, one of the most distinguished medals for bravery in the French Army. He devoted himself to the republican values of France.

Of course the values of France do not simply consist of republican values. There is the moral universalism that Fanon espoused, but there is also a strain of reactionary politics that has haunted France for centuries. De Gaulle's Free France was fighting against the collaborationist regime of Marshal Pétain. Fanon's schoolteacher admonished anti-Semitism, but France was also the nation that wrongly convicted a Jewish man, Alfred Dreyfus, of treason. France has a distinct tradition of reactionary thought, from the eighteenth-century arch-conservative philosopher Joseph de Maistre to the far-right poet and thinker Charles Maurras; from the novelist Louis-Ferdinand Céline to the politician Jean-Marie Le Pen. The French Revolution abolished slavery in its colonies, but the successor to the revolution, Napoleon Bonaparte, brought it back. In more recent years, the 1998 France World Cup team won the major competition of the most popular sport in the world on home soil; but many of the black players on the team encountered racism from other French people on their way to doing so. The point is not to say that either one of these types of politics is any more French than the other, but to emphasize that they are all refracted through French history and culture. The same is true of Fanon. He was born in Martinique, devoted his life to Algeria and died in America, but his thoughts and ideas reflected the influence of France. To truly understand him, we need to look at Fanon in terms of this cultural context, rather than translating him out of it.

* * *

When black Americans are not seen for their context, in the ways outlined by Ellison and Murray, they turn from living beings into bloodless *notions*. They become *invisible*: so much is lost in the attempt to translate their complex lived experiences into simplistic concepts. Instead of Jeffrey, thirty-five, from Atlanta, an accountant with a wife and three kids, who loves grits and Marvel movies and may or may not like hip-hop music, you simply have a *black man*. Everything human about him has been dried out. Just as to understand French (or any other language) you need to understand the language on its own terms, so the same is true of racial identity. You need to see black Americans through their own distinctive set of experiences and cultures, not through a lens that simply reduces them to their race. When Baldwin confidently said to Angelou that he was an American, he was – like Ellison's protagonist – asserting his visibility: the fact that he was more than simply a black man. He was a fundamental part of America. This is the case for integrationism.

3

CRITICAL RACE THEORY

Malcolm X thought black people were not Americans, and he dismissed the notion of racial progress: 'You don't stick a knife in a man's back nine inches and then pull it out six inches and say you're making progress.'[1] He embodied the tradition of black nationalism. Elaine Brown, former chairwoman of the Black Panther Party, has also argued against integration and insisted on seeing black people in America as a separate nation. In a 1993 round-table discussion on the condition of race in America, she claimed that 'we are still Africans lost in America as far as I'm concerned, and we do have to address our issues on our own because I don't believe there is an agenda for assimilation'. She added that 'I don't want to be assimilated into an environment that has committed genocide on other peoples, that has endorsed chattel slavery and institutional oppression.'[2] For Brown, there has been little progress since the Civil Rights Movement, and the only way for black Americans to protect their dignity is by affirming their blackness.

Stokely Carmichael, Malcolm's successor as the leading radical voice of black activism, was also at that conference. By this time he was a member of the All-African People's Revolutionary Party and now referred to black Americans as simply Africans. As he put it in a 1989 television interview, 'I do not even use the term African-American. I use the term Africans, because that's what we are. We are Africans in America. There is nothing American about us. Our history has only been a history of struggle in America.' And that struggle is never-ending unless, according to Carmichael, capitalism is overthrown. The enduring presence of capitalism is why there is no progress for black people in America.

Today, the way of thinking that discounts progress in race relations manifests itself most clearly in critical race theory and one of its offshoots: intersectionality. Ultimately, though, this chapter argues that even these concepts, which ostensibly reject many aspects of America, can't be comprehended without an understanding of American culture, politics and history. These ideas are still as American as apple pie.

Ta-Nehisi Coates is the most distinguished black American intellectual during the second decade of the twenty-first century. His 2015 book, *Between the World and Me*, won the National Book Award for Nonfiction; Toni Morrison anointed him as James Baldwin's successor; Coates used to be a national correspondent for *The Atlantic* magazine; and the publication of his essays is a national event. Coates is a pessimist about the American Dream: like Malcolm X, he believes that any commitment to it betrays a naive attitude to the gruesome reality of American racism. 'There is nothing uniquely evil' about racists in America, Coates argues: they 'are merely men enforcing the whims of our country, correctly interpreting its heritage and legacy'.[3] Racism is not a blemish on the country. It is an integral part of America.

For Coates, the Civil Rights Movement has ultimately been a failure: 'I could see that some fifty years after the civil rights movement black people could still be found at the bottom of virtually every socioeconomic metric of note.'[4] This pessimistic tone – believing that the American project of ensuring liberty and equality for all citizens is a sham, and that America is in existential conflict with its black citizens – was shared by a little-known intellectual who established the concept that is now discussed across much of America and the world today. His name also appeared in that 1993 conference, along with Brown and Carmichael, during which he argued that 'Notwithstanding the advances and the changes, the fact is equal opportunity has rendered us in many ways worse off than we were under separate but equal [the formulation that underpinned legal segregation in America].' According to this man, when there is a conflict of interests between black Americans and wider American society, black Americans will always lose out. His name was Derrick Bell, and he was one of the founders of critical race theory.

Bell wasn't a firebrand. He didn't dress stylishly or speak charismatically. He was a mild-mannered college professor with a slightly whimsical voice. He was born in 1930, and in 1971 he became the first black American to be a tenured professor at Harvard Law School. His rise was meteoric: neither of his parents had attended college. Bell himself had studied at the relatively undistinguished Duquesne University in Pennsylvania.[5] The central argument of critical race theory – the doctrine that he spent many years creating – is that racism is a permanent feature of American life. It is not an aberration. It is not an accident. It is woven into the fabric of the nation: in society, in the government, in schools, in courts and at work. This view, which would have seemed rather extreme in the past, is now mainstream in many parts of academia and the liberal-left media, as a response to high-profile instances of police shooting black men, greater attention paid to mass incarceration, and the emergence of Donald Trump. It has also been promoted in higher education and has spread through social media.

In their introductory textbook, *Critical Race Theory*, Richard Delgado and Jean Stefancic, two Bell disciples, explain that 'unlike traditional civil rights, which embraces incrementalism and step-by-step progress, critical race theory questions the very foundations of the liberal order'.[6] For Martin Luther King and, later, Barack Obama and their fellow integrationists, American racism was the consequence of the country failing to live up to the principles of its constitution. For Bell and advocates of critical race theory, these very principles are rotten to the core; the people who wrote these ideas in the constitution assumed that black people were inferior.

Bell was an unlikely candidate for being the father of critical race theory. When he was young he worked for the NAACP, the establishment anti-racism group that believed American society could be transformed through the legal system. But he became disillusioned with the power of the law to change society. The key historical moment in critical race theory was not the abolition of slavery or the passing of the Civil Rights Act in 1964, which brought an end to segregation in public places. It was the 1954 Supreme Court ruling, after the *Brown v. Board of Education* case, which found that 'separate but equal' public schooling was unconstitutional. The ruling proclaimed that segregation in public schooling violated the Fourteenth Amendment – which, after former slaves were granted citizenship following the American Civil War, had affirmed that all citizens possessed 'equal protection of the laws'.[7] If black Americans have separate schooling, they are hindered from achieving the equality enshrined in law.

Many standard textbooks on the history of the Civil Rights Movement view *Brown v. Board* as the start of the civil-rights revolution, which concluded a decade later in the 1964 Civil Rights Act and the 1965 Voting Rights Act. But the founding father of critical race theory was sceptical about the impact of this ruling. In fact he thought it was a big swindle. In an article published in the *Harvard Law Review* in 1980, Bell argued that the decision was based on: 'value to whites, not simply those concerned about the immorality of racial inequality, but also those whites in policymaking positions able to see the economic and political advances at home and abroad that would follow abandonment of segregation'.[8]

In other words, the decision was motivated by cynical self-interest rather than a genuine wish to fulfil

America's founding principles. Domestic legislation in the fifties was shadowed by the Cold War – and, in the battle against communism, America wanted to be seen as morally superior. The United States did not want to play into communist propaganda, which depicted it as a country twisted by hypocrisy, preaching equality but practising hatred.

Bell's critique of *Brown v. Board*, however, went deeper than a condemnation of hypocrisy and self-interest. He was a realist rather than an idealist. He believed that a few laws do not change 250 years of slavery followed by 100 years of segregation and violent terror. 'My position,' he wrote in his 1992 text *Faces at the Bottom of the Well*, 'is that the legal rules regarding racial discrimination have become not only reified (that is, ascribing material existence and power to what are really just ideas) but deified.'[9] In mythologizing America's campaign against racism, we lose sight of what is really going on: the persistence of racial inequalities under different guises. Sure, it is illegal to not hire a person on the basis of his race; lynching is a thing of the past; and you can marry across races. But there are still stark racial inequalities in American society: today white Americans are ten times wealthier than black Americans; black Americans are far more likely to be locked up in prison.

But Bell was a realist in another sense, too. He thought moral considerations and sentiments should not get in the way of dispassionate analysis. Sentiment is dangerous because it can lead to delusion and can operate at the expense of moral reasoning. As he expressed it, 'the worship of equality rules as having absolute power' – one of the distinguishing features of American culture – 'benefits whites by preserving a benevolent but fictional self-image, and such worship benefits blacks by preserving hope.'[10]

Hope sustains the dreams of many black Americans. The alternative is too painful. It is also contrary to the deeply ingrained intuitions of American citizens of all races: that the world can be completely transformed, that a moral wrong can be conclusively turned into a right. America has historically been seen as a beacon of hope. As the American historian Jennifer Ratner-Rosenhagen puts it, European observers thought 'if ever there was a place in the world where such a sublime thing could exist' as in the Elysian Fields, then 'America was it.'[11] John Locke, the influential English philosopher, said of America: 'Thus in the beginning all the World was America.' Thomas Paine invoked the image of Noah's Ark when he wrote this of America in 1776: 'A situation, similar to the present, hath not happened since the days of Noah until now. The birthday of a new world is at hand.'

America, in this mythologized picture, stands as an exception and a model to the rest of the world. Hope is what animated the politics of Martin Luther King, and it found its most stirring expression in his 'I Have a Dream' speech. Hope also shaped the politics of Barack Obama; he even titled his second book *The Audacity of Hope: Thoughts on Reclaiming the American Dream*. Obama loved Martin Luther King's quote – 'the arc of the moral universe is long, but it bends toward justice' – so much that he cited it thirty-three times as president.[12] King himself got the quote from a nineteenth-century abolitionist preacher called Theodore Parker. It is a part of the American moral furniture. But Bell was having none of this.

For Bell, hope was a hindrance. 'I think,' he writes, that 'we've arrived at a place in history where the harms of such worship', of equality and fairness, 'outweigh its benefit'. Those who persist in clinging on to the vision of the nation as a bastion of enlightened values are not only naive; they are complicit in propping up a dangerous illusion.[13]

This disenchantment with America's ideals may make Bell seem like Ta-Nehisi Coates's intellectual predecessor. But unlike Coates, who believed the arc of history bends towards chaos rather than justice, and that there was no underlying meaning to human existence, Bell saw things very differently. He was not an atheist. He was a Christian. In his book *Ethical Ambition*, which mixes memoir and self-help, he emphasized that 'humanity at its essence is both an ongoing readiness to recognize wrongs and try to make things better, and the desire to help those in need of assistance without expecting reward or public recognition.'[14]

This combination of attention to how bad things are, along with a desire to make them better, recalls James Baldwin. In the closing passage of Baldwin's essay 'Notes of a Native Son' he writes that, 'it began to seem to me that one would have to hold in the mind forever two ideas which seemed to be in opposition. The first idea was acceptance of life as it is, and men as they are: in light of this idea, it goes without saying that injustice is a commonplace.'[15] The second idea was equally valuable: 'one must never, in one's life, accept these injustices as commonplace but must fight them with all one's strength.' Bell took on this challenge, and one way to reconcile these two sides of him – the moralist and the pessimist – is to emphasize his Christianity. He believed in the permanence of racism, just as any Christian believes in the existence of sin. Nevertheless, the existence of evil does not mean that we shouldn't do good. The fact that we are irreducibly imperfect shouldn't stop us from striving to make the world a better place.

I think a better way to account for this tension is to view Bell's conception of critical race theory as a consequence of a deeply ingrained Americanism rather than as a rejection of it. Bell still believed in American exceptionalism. America did not become a post-racial utopia after the civil-rights revolution, Bell would argue, and therefore racism is an ineradicable feature of American society. But the standards by which he was judging America are not neutral ones, but the very standards that American patriots claim to consecrate: equality and fairness and liberty. Bell was still attached to these criteria. His disenchantment still had an American flavour. Just as a vocal and aggressive atheist is often in some sense an inverted believer, so men like Bell and Coates – so antagonistic to American idealism – belie their underlying attachment to it.

Coates's criticism of America is animated by his acceptance of its exceptionalism. 'One cannot,' he writes, 'at once, claim to be superhuman and then plead mortal error.' His proposal is this: 'to take our countrymen's claims of American exceptionalism seriously, which is to say I propose subjecting our country to an exceptional moral standard'.[16] In other words, despite his cynical rhetoric about America,

THIS IS NOT AMERICA

Coates seems to take at face value the ideals of the American Dream rather than wholly rejecting them. In this sense, the comparison that Toni Morrison made between him and Baldwin ultimately made sense.

Meanwhile, conservative opponents of critical race theory see it as fundamentally un-American. Activists like Christopher Rufo complain that critical race theory has 'pervaded every aspect of the federal government' and poses 'an existential threat to the United States'.[17] He calls the teaching of the ideology in schools an example of state-sanctioned racism. Others, like the American author James Lindsay, compare critical race theory to Marxism – an alien ideology that threatens America, just like communism during the Cold War.[18] The truth is that critical race theory is an American ideology. It ultimately espouses some of the nation's self-professed values. If such values are as fundamentally corrupt as Bell and Coates say they are, why subject America to the standards of these values in the first place? The visions of the shining city on a hill, of manifest destiny, of a providential nation that will bring about liberty and equality for all, become the metric by which they judge the nation. And this metric is an American one, reflecting as it does the series of ideas that have been turned over and over again by American thinkers and citizens since its inception. The fact that it is a myth is beside the point. All nations are founded on myths; all nations are founded on forgetting inconvenient facts. As Ernest Renan, the French historian, famously said of nations, 'Getting its history wrong is part of being a nation.'[19] But the hostility by Coates and Bell to this self-mythologizing aspect of America is itself an American form of hostility. As James Baldwin affirms: 'I love America more than any other country in this world, and exactly for this reason, I insist on the right to criticize her perpetually.'

* * *

Critical race theory is also American in another sense: it reflects the nation's obsession with race. One way to think about this more deeply is to consider the related concept of intersectionality. The term 'intersectionality' was coined by the American legal scholar Kimberlé Crenshaw in 1989 to describe how various forms of oppression overlap with one another. This sounds reasonable enough. Sexism, for example, shouldn't be seen in a vacuum. A woman may be oppressed simply on the basis of her sex, but if that woman is also black, then she can be burdened by racism, too. Crenshaw's

1989 paper was entitled 'Demarginalizing the Intersection of Race and Sex: A Black Feminist Critique of Antidiscrimination Doctrine, Feminist Theory and Antiracist Politics'.[20] Her paper was an analysis of three legal cases in which a black woman is discriminated against in terms of both her race and sex. The problem with all these cases, Crenshaw argues, is the 'conceptual limitations' of 'single-issue analyses'. By this, she means that when we think about oppression, we often think about racism and sexism and classism and homophobia as separate forces, when in fact they often interact to compound the oppression experienced by an individual. She writes that 'in race discrimination cases, discrimination tends to be viewed in terms of sex- or class-privileged Blacks; in sex discrimination cases, the focus is on race- and class-privileged women'. The only way to properly challenge this system of interlocking oppression, according to Crenshaw, is through radical change rather than reform. In a profile of her for the website Vox, the American journalist Jane Coaston writes: 'In short, Crenshaw doesn't want to replicate existing power dynamics and cultural structures just to give people of color power over white people, for example. She wants to get rid of those existing power dynamics altogether – changing the very structures that undergird our politics, law, and culture in order to level the playing field.'[21]

Like Bell, Crenshaw is sceptical about the power of legislation to get rid of racism. It is too deeply enmeshed in American society for lawmakers to banish it. In an essay for *The Baffler* in 2017, she writes of old-fashioned civil-rights lawyers that 'they shared a baseline confidence that once the irrational distortions of bias were removed, the underlying legal and socioeconomic order would revert to a neutral, benign state of impersonally apportioned justice'.[22] Crenshaw is opposed to a 'colour-blind' approach to racism: one that affirms that we need to be neutral on matters of race and make it irrelevant, if we want to get rid of racial discrimination. For her, a neutral attitude to race serves only to justify a pre-existing racist social order. Being neutral on racism won't serve the young black men who are incarcerated; the black women with worse health outcomes; the black people living in poverty.

Although she writes and speaks notably about black Americans, Crenshaw affirms that white supremacy harms all minorities. It not only harms the black American descendant of slaves; it also harms the Hispanic migrant who is treated as a drain on resources, and the Arab Muslim migrant who is suspected of being a terrorist. In a debate hosted by the British organization, the Institute of Art and Ideas, she argues that 'the challenge is to have a conversation about race and racism that's sophisticated enough to deal with the fact that white supremacy is very sophisticated'.[23] According to her, white supremacy 'can distinguish different groups and it can exclude them in different ways' and can 'still maintain itself as the primary desired category to be. And it aggregates power in a way that allows it to produce these different outcomes for various groups.' There's not one story of racism, but 'white supremacy plays out across these different moments'. White supremacy has many tentacles.

The problem with intersectionality is that it is not intersectional enough. By this, I mean it is too narrow in its analysis of inequalities. As the American writer Coleman Hughes puts it: 'It's not clear that black women are worse off than black men. Yes, black women are far more likely to suffer domestic violence and rape. But black men are far more likely to suffer incarceration, murder, and suicide.'[24] Black men were also far more likely to be lynched than black women during the Jim Crow era. Which is not to say that black men are *more* oppressed than black women. Hughes's point is that it's not self-evidently true that either group is more oppressed than the other.

Hughes also accuses Crenshaw of committing the

'disparity fallacy' – the idea that all the social problems of black Americans can be explained by racism. The disparity fallacy has been pointed out by black Americans of varying ideological persuasions. It is not simply a right-wing talking point. Hughes is himself a liberal. Thomas Sowell, one of the most prominent debunkers of the disparity fallacy, is a conservative economist. 'The assumption that discriminatory bias can be automatically inferred when there are differences in socioeconomic outcomes,' according to Sowell, 'seems indefensible. Yet that seemingly invincible fallacy guides much of what is said and done in our educational institutions, in the media, and in government policies.'[25] But someone who also criticized the disparity fallacy was the progressive campaigner Bayard Rustin, who introduced the philosophy of non-violence to Martin Luther King and was one of the main architects of the March on Washington. In one essay he argued that 'It would be convenient to ascribe all the problems confronting black Americans to the persistence of racism.'[26] But this was not the case: 'while racism continues to exert a baneful influence upon our society,' he added, 'the plight of black Americans today is more and more the consequence of a number of important nonracist, structural features of our economy'. These included, among other things:

The decline in labor-intensive industries and the displacement of unskilled and semiskilled black workers as a consequence of automation and robotization… The elimination, because of unfair foreign competition and a severe recession, of hundreds of thousands of jobs in industries such as steel and autos that have historically provided wellpaying jobs for large numbers of black workers.

Within intersectionality there is also a tension between presenting white supremacy as a force that harms all minorities and the fact that many minorities in America are succeeding in areas that are used to explain why there is white supremacy in the first place. So the fact that black Americans are struggling in schools, in work and in the criminal justice system is adduced to explain the pernicious force of white supremacy. But Asian-Americans are performing so well in education that in 2014 an organization called Students for Fair Admissions sued Harvard because they thought they were discriminated against by affirmative-action policies.[27] Some African and Caribbean immigrant communities are over-represented in education. In other words, intersectionality is still tied to the American myth of black people at the bottom of the hierarchy and white people at the top. This may be true of America's past, and is still to a great extent true today, but it's not absolutely true. It doesn't account for many of the other minorities in America, and it should not be assumed to be true across the rest of the world – including Britain.

* * *

The most prominent advocates for the ideas of critical race theory today are a white American woman, a British-raised woman who lives in Qatar and a black American man: Robin DiAngelo, Layla F. Saad and Ibram X. Kendi respectively. Their books are not only popular in America, but in Europe too. However, they still derive from an American context: an American style of self-help book.

Robin DiAngelo was born in San Jose, California, her parents separated when she was young, and she moved apartments several times a year because her single mother couldn't pay the rent and bills. Her mother also couldn't afford the medical and dental care for DiAngelo and her sisters. Robin was bullied at school for being poor. When she was eleven, her mother died of leukaemia and she was sent to live with her father. But by the summer of 2020, very soon after George Floyd's murder, her book *White Fragility* had become the bestselling book on Amazon: it sold so many copies that it soon ran out of stock. She became one of the most influential public intellectuals in America. From rags to riches, from marginal to mainstream, her very life story reflects many of the myths that are central to America's conception of itself – and her ideas are no different.

She received her BA in her mid-thirties at Seattle University and her PhD in the field of multicultural education more than a decade later from Washington University. It was between her undergraduate degree and her doctorate that she qualified as a diversity trainer, for which she would become famous. A diversity trainer is someone who advises businesses and communities on how to positively interact with black and ethnic-minority people. It was out of this work that DiAngelo created the concept and title of her first bestseller: *White Fragility*.

'White fragility' means that white people are unable to discuss race and racism without feeling anxious and defensive. They feel like they are being personally judged. As a result, they don't want to even touch on the conversation. In a way, this is quite understandable: nobody wants to be thought of as a bad person. But racism is about power. It is an ideology that enforces the superiority of white people at the expense of black and brown people. So anti-racist white people need to 'build' their own 'racial stamina' in order to endure these uncomfortable conversations about race and racism.[28] White fragility, however, is not a benign or neutral force: 'it is a powerful means of white racial control and the protection of white advantage'. Saying, 'I'm not personally a racist' is a cop-out. By personalizing racism, this distracts us from trying to identify and challenge its true nature: as a structural force. The genius of DiAngelo's argument is that anyone hostile to, or even sceptical about, it can fall into what is called the Kafka Trap: if you reject her thesis, this is proof that it is correct, because you are demonstrating white fragility. The only option is to acquiesce. If you are white, that is.

DiAngelo's book *Nice Racism: How Progressive White People Perpetuate Racial Harm*, was published in 2021, a year after the summer of racial reckoning. Her target audience was progressive white people. Such people are generally on the left, but they can also be moderates, centrists and even soft conservatives. They probably read *The Root* or *The New York Times* and, as she puts it in her book, they 'listen to NPR or the BBC as they commute to their job at a non-profit or tech company'. They can be of any age. And they typically live in large urban cities or smaller progressive enclaves.[29] The problem with white progressives, DiAngelo argues, is that they are more likely to locate racism in other white people than in themselves. She suggests that white progressives present a clearer threat to black people than white supremacists, because black people are unlikely to encounter white supremacists in their day-to-day lives. By contrast, 'We are the ones – with a smile on our faces – who undermine Black people daily in ways both harder to identify and easier to deny.'

Crucially, DiAngelo doesn't think the younger generation is less racist than older white people. 'The young white people I work with in cities such as New York and Oakland don't actually lead integrated lives, despite the racial diversity that may surround them. This diversity is often the temporary result of the process of gentrification.' Destructive white progressive patterns include unconvincing credentialling (I'm not a racist – I grew up in a diverse area), racial ignorance, a lack of racial humility, an inability to hold racial discomfort and the entitlement to take up space. But unlike *White Fragility*, *Nice Racism* has a greater focus on practical solutions.[30]

Her practical solutions include, among other things, attending white affinity groups. This is when a group of white people meet together to discuss their internalized superiority, implicit bias, guilt, confusion and resentment, and do this in a racially segregated space in order not to cause harm to black and brown people. Another solution that she recommends is getting accountability partners of colour – people who have agreed to coach you, think with you and challenge you on your inevitable racism; and they should be paid for this. You should also, to get the full experience, seek white accountability partners. DiAngelo says that she doesn't offer to pay her white friends for this, but she generously informs us, 'there are white people with strong analysis and deep experience who do offer professional aid coaching'.[31] In other words, her recommendation is a form of self-help.

But there is a basic incoherence at the heart of DiAngelo's argument. She argues that every white person is socialized to be racist, and it is thus up to white individuals themselves to personally undo this by building up their own racial stamina. But she also claims that she has no truck with the ideology of individualism: racism is a structural problem, not an individual one, and the only way to undo it is through structural means rather than individual ones. Ultimately, however, what is most striking is the individualism at the heart of her thinking. DiAngelo's books are not utopian manifestoes or radical Marxist tracts. They are the most American of genres: self-help books. *White Fragility* and *Nice Racism* are self-help books for white people who want to know how to fight racism. Or for white people who want to feel as though they're fighting racism.

In an essay for *The New Yorker* on the resonance of self-help books in American society, the cultural critic Louis Menand posits that 'Since the United States was founded on the principle of "no aristocracy of birth," which was supposed to distinguish the New World from the Old, it makes sense that how-to and self-help should be central to American life – and that a book about those books should be called "Americanon."'[32]

DiAngelo's books are part of this Americanon. They are concerned with transforming your individual character to make you a more virtuous and enlightened person. In two other books that are often sold alongside hers – Layla F. Saad's *Me and White Supremacy* and Ibram X. Kendi's *How to Be an Antiracist* – readers are encouraged to use a journal when reading the main text. They are going on an individual journey, and the purpose of the journal is to track the progress of this journey. It is like a Puritan recording his or her spiritual struggles in a diary.

Saad's book began as a twenty-eight-day Instagram challenge. It then became a PDF workbook that was downloaded by more than 100,000 people around the world. It is written as a companion guide for white readers to unpack their complicity in white supremacy. Saad has never lived in America; she was born and bred in Britain and currently lives in Qatar. But this does not stop her using a term like BIPOC (black, indigenous and people of colour) to refer to ethnic-minority people generally. Like all successful self-help authors, she knows her audience: they are either American or have internalized American culture to such an extent that they can read about the marginalization of 'indigenous communities' without blinking an eye – even if, for instance, they live in Europe, where the defence of 'indigenous communities' carries with it a more sinister resonance. Throughout the book, moreover, there is no mention that she currently resides in a state that imports slave labour from South Asia and persecutes gay people: some forms of oppression apparently matter more than others.

Like DiAngelo, Saad is interested in specifically addressing the individual: 'For the purposes of this book,' she writes, 'we are only going to be exploring and unpacking what white supremacy looks like at the personal and individual level.' She sounds like a gunnery sergeant from a Stanley Kubrick epic: 'There are no safety nets, no shortcuts, and no easier routes. You will want to close the book, run away, and pretend you never heard of me,' she instructs her reader. 'You will want to blame me, rage at me, discredit me, and list all the reasons why you are a good person and why you don't need to do this work. That is a normal, expected response. That is the response of the white fragility and anti-Blackness lying inside.'[33] But you can, of course, overcome this. Only listen and do everything your teacher tells you to do. Like an old-fashioned textbook, there are questions at the end of each chapter for the reader to answer in order to measure how much progress she or he is making.

Meanwhile, Ibram X. Kendi's *How to Be an Antiracist* is distinct from many contemporary anti-racist books in one important way: he believes black people can also be racist towards white people. As a college student, Kendi briefly thought white people were aliens. He no longer believes this. 'Whenever someone classifies people of European descent as biologically, culturally, or behaviourally inferior,' he writes, 'whenever someone says there is something wrong with White people as a group, someone is articulating a racist idea.'[34] Would this mean that those who say all white people are racist – as DiAngelo and Saad do – are themselves racist? According to Kendi's definition, the answer would have to be yes. Indeed, definitions are absolutely critical for Kendi.

Like a Victorian taxonomist, he fanatically delineates between categories. He wants clear and consistent definitions of terms like racist and anti-racist: 'If we don't do the basic work of defining the kind of people we want to be in language that is stable and consistent,' he writes, 'we can't work toward stable, consistent goals.' For Kendi, a racist is someone 'who is supporting a racist policy through their actions or inaction or expressing a racist idea'. And an anti-racist is someone 'who is supporting an anti-racist policy through their actions or expressing an anti-racist idea'.[35] But what's a racist policy? It is anything that produces or sustains racial inequity. And racial inequity is when 'two or more racial groups are not standing on approximately equal footing'. So, for example, the fact that 70 per cent of white families lived in owner-occupied homes in 2014, compared to 45 per cent Hispanic families and 41 per cent of black families, is a consequence of racist policy and nothing else. The alternative, according to Kendi, would be implying that it is the fault of black and Hispanic people that they are less likely to own their homes.

Clear and consistent definitions are good. Too many of these discussions rely upon vaguely defined concepts. But Kendi is too reductive in his analysis of racism. He splits everything down the middle.

For him, there is no such thing as a race-neutral policy. Every policy either produces or challenges racial inequities. And there is no such thing as being a non-racist. If you don't subscribe to the view that racial inequities are a product of policy decisions and nothing else, then you are complicit in racism. 'The opposite of "racist,"' Kendi writes, 'isn't non-racist. It is "anti-racist."' One who 'believes problems are rooted in groups of people', rather than in power and policies, 'is a racist'. The fact that Ghanaian-Americans and Nigerian-Americans earn more than native-born black Americans, for instance, is itself a product of racism. West African immigrants who compare themselves favourably to the native black population are engaged in ethnic racism. The fact that Indian-Americans and Chinese-Americans are similarly affluent is also a consequence of nothing other than racism. Cultural norms and economic differences mask what, to Kendi's mind, ought to be clear and obvious: the unbending reality of racism. In fact it's not clear and obvious at all, unless your mind is so bound up with race that nothing else truly matters in explaining society.

How can we get rid of racist discrimination? DiAngelo and Saad are vague on this. Kendi has a clear answer: 'The only remedy to racist discrimination is anti-racist discrimination.' According to Kendi, discrimination is not necessarily bad; it just depends on whether it is about helping a disadvantaged group or making its lot worse. This is part of his rejection of race-neutral policy: 'The most threatening racist movement,' he writes, 'is not the alt right's [a loosely connected white supremacist and white nationalist movement] unlikely drive for a White ethnostate but the regular American's drive for a "race neutral" one.' Linked to this opposition to race neutrality is Kendi's hostility to judging communities and cultures by a common set of moral standards. 'To be antiracist,' he writes, 'is to see all cultures in all their differences as on the same level, as equals. When we see cultural difference, we see cultural difference – nothing more, nothing less.'[36] That Kendi doesn't entertain the obvious moral objections to this claim – that a culture that engages in female genital mutilation, for example, is not on the same moral level as one that forbids such a practice; that a society that hangs gay people from cranes is not morally equivalent to one that allows them to marry other gay people; that a country that celebrates diversity is not the same as one that imports slave labour – speaks to his fascinatingly perverse dogmatism. Moral universalism (the view that there are universal moral laws, and they should apply irrespectively of cultural norms and practices) is presented as another example of white supremacy.

The irony in aligning culture so strictly to people (so that to condemn a cultural practice is to condemn the people who engage in it) is that it reflects a long-standing racist trope: that black people and the positive norms associated with Western culture are incompatible. But Kendi is wrong on this. Cultures don't have rights; people do.

For Kendi, however, being a racist is not the worst thing in the world. 'It is not the worst word in the English language; it is not the equivalent of a slur,' he writes. 'It is descriptive, and the only way to undo racism is to consistently identify and describe it – and then dismantle it. The attempt to turn this usefully descriptive term into an almost unusable slur is, of course, designed to do the opposite: to freeze us into inaction.'[37] But racism is a stigma. The reason why this is the case is that Western society has elevated it into a grave moral wrong. But Kendi is effectively saying to his reader, as DiAngelo does with her concept of white fragility: get over yourselves. Don't be squeamish. This coldness is inhuman. How can we fight against racial injustice if we strip racism of its moral content and treat it in such a bloodless way? Should we, in fact, de-stigmatize racism? At times, Kendi writes like a robot; his arguments are utterly detached from the textures of reality. His book is characterized by an all-consuming racial obsession, and this obsession is an American one.

Black American integrationism is American; black nationalism in America is American; critical race theory is also American. All of these ideas are influenced by the United States: one wouldn't be able to understand them without understanding the particular history and ideals of America. In the case of American integrationism, it is American because the writers are explicitly invoking American ideals to condemn racism. In the case of black nationalism and critical race theory, they implicitly invoke American ideals. The frame of reference is still American: they still accept American exceptionalism, obsess in an American way about race and popularize their ideas through an American style of self-help. In order to have a better understanding of the debates on race in America, and the ideas that emerge from these debates, we thus need to judge them on American terms. We should not view them through a neutral perspective.

Part 2

THIS IS BRITAIN

4

IMMIGRATION

Black Americans have more in common with white Americans than they do with black people across the rest of the world. We know this insight to be true by observing the wisdom of Ralph Ellison and James Baldwin. And if we accept this, we have to accept something equally important: black British people have more in common with other British people than they do with black people across the rest of the world. We need to be integrationist in a British sense. We must not make black British people invisible.

Black British people are British. To understand them we need to understand British society and history, and one thing is clear from any attention paid to the evidence: race doesn't define British society in the same way it defines American society. Jim Crow-style segregation has never been enforced in Britain. My family, and the majority of black people in the

UK, arrived as immigrants. The story of black people in Britain is the immigrant experience, and it is by understanding this that we can better understand black British identity. This chapter explores post-Second World War immigration to Britain, the first substantial influx of black migrants to the UK, and argues that the case against racism in Britain is strengthened by emphasizing the connection that black British people have with Britain, rather than seeing them for their race alone.

Marlene Headley was born in London in the late 1950s to two immigrants from Jamaica: Mildred and Gladstone Headley. Mildred worked for London Transport and later trained as a nurse. Gladstone worked for British Rail. Marlene grew up in Kilburn, north London, listening to the music of her parents' cultural background – calypso, reggae, ska. But her father also introduced her to the Nigerian musician Fela Kuti, and this gave Marlene her first connection to Africa. She has described how 'the programme *Roots* is how I found out I got here, how I found how the rest of the world sees us'.[1]

Roots was a television programme from the 1970s that was adapted from a novel by Alex Haley, in which an African named Kunta Kinte is enslaved and transported to America, and we see his progeny down the ages. Marlene felt an attachment to Africa. This grew when she was eighteen and moved to Hackney to study community studies. While she was there she discovered an African dance group and was totally enraptured: 'To hear Africans with strong accents, learn about the food and the drumming touched my heart and took me to a place I had never been. It was everything for me and I had never felt so free as when I was listening to those drums.' She adds that 'my connection with Africa became my lifelong story. It's identity, because ours was robbed from us. Overtime, Black people have been forced to try and be something they are not.' Marlene Headley later founded an organization called Sistah Space. It is a charity that helps black British women who have suffered domestic or sexual abuse. She also changed her name to Ngozi Fulani: Ngozi is a traditional Igbo name and Fulani is a West African ethnic group. In November 2022 Ngozi was attending a charity event at Buckingham Palace and encountered Lady Susan Hussey, who had been lady-in-waiting to Queen Elizabeth II for more than sixty years and is godmother to Prince William. Ngozi was wearing an African dress. According to her, their conversation ran something like this:[2]

Lady SH: Where are you from?
Ngozi: Sistah Space.

SH: No, where do you come from?

Ngozi: We're based in Hackney.

SH: No, what part of Africa are you from?

Ngozi: I don't know, they didn't leave any records.

SH: Well, you must know where you're from, I spent time in France. Where are you from?

Ngozi: Here, the UK.

SH: No, but what nationality are you?

Ngozi: I am born here and am British.

SH: No, but where do you really come from, where do your people come from?

Ngozi: 'My people', lady, what is this?

SH: Oh I can see I am going to have a challenge getting you to say where you're from. When did you first come here?

Ngozi: Lady! I am a British national, my parents came here in the fifties when...

SH: Oh, I knew we'd get there in the end, you're Caribbean!

Ngozi: No lady, I am of African heritage, Caribbean descent and British nationality.

SH: Oh so you're from...

Ngozi Fulani, who had changed her name and proudly wore an African dress, who identified so strongly with Africa in these and so many other senses, was now insisting on a British identity in the face of invasive questioning by Lady Susan Hussey. The striking point was that Hussey swiftly resigned after the incident; a consensus quickly developed that this was an instance of institutional racism. The anti-racist response from everyone was predicated on the conviction that Ngozi Fulani (or Marlene Headley) is British. That she is not African. Otherwise Lady Susan Hussey's question would have been benign. The query that she might not be British can't be understood, moreover, without understanding that black British communities are an immigrant population in a way that black Americans are not.

* * *

I was born with an African name and in an African country. I grew up in Plumstead and Eltham and went to secondary school in Kidbrooke. This patch of south-east London is my home; it is where I first developed a sense of belonging to Britain. Other black people have settled in this area of London before – and with that sense of belonging. One of them was a boy called Stephen Lawrence. He wanted to be an architect, but he never fulfilled his dream because he was stabbed to death by a gang of white supremacists in 1993. He was nineteen. I say this not to state that my life is like Lawrence's. This would be offensive to his memory and untrue. I say it rather to emphasize the fact that any honest reckoning of black lives in Britain needs also to account for the deadly racism that has plagued the lives of many black people in Britain. This is part of the story too.

Lawrence lived in Plumstead and was killed in Eltham. I knew of him when I was a boy. And I knew violent racism of that particular kind was a feature of Britain's past. But I didn't know until a few years after I had left Eltham that I grew up just a stroll away from an attack that would powerfully transform race legislation in Britain – leading, for instance, to the 1999 Macpherson Report that established a working definition of institutional racism.[3] I lived in a state of innocence. I was ignorant of the racist history of the area I was inhabiting. But I lived in an even more fundamental sense of innocence: virtually all the white people I encountered on the streets of southeast London were kind to me. It was my home, and it felt like it. But it has also been the home of so many other black people; and they have been made to feel like they are strangers. One dimension of the history of black people in Britain is this tension between belonging and alienation, between Britain as the motherland and the land of estrangement.

Paulette Wilson had been living in Britain for almost fifty years and rightly thought of herself as British. But in 2015 she was made to feel like a foreigner and told to go home – not by a drunk racist on the bus on a Friday night, but by a letter sent to her address from an arm of the British state: the Home Office. Paulette was born in the British colony of Jamaica in 1956. When she was ten she boarded a plane alone and moved to Britain. Her mother sent her so that Paulette could go and live with her grandparents. Paulette never visited Jamaica again; she never saw her mum again. She lived, studied and worked in Britain, raising a child and a grandchild, working as a cook in the House of Commons and volunteering in her local church to serve meals to homeless people. She had been paying National Insurance contributions for thirty-four years when she was designated an illegal immigrant, sent to the Yarl's Wood detention centre and taken to the immigration removal unit at Heathrow airport. Her life and dedication to this country – it seemed – had been worth nothing. She would be cut off from her home and family. She told the *Guardian* journalist Amelia Gentleman that when she spent that week in Yarl's Wood, 'I felt like I didn't exist. I wondered what was going to happen to me. All I did was cry, thinking of my daughter and granddaughter; thinking that

I wasn't going to see them again.'[4] A last-minute intervention from her MP, Emma Reynolds, and a local charity saved Paulette from being deported to a country she had only known as a small child. The letter from the Home Office should never have been sent in the first place.

The 1971 Immigration Act gave Commonwealth immigrants who had already settled in Britain the right to indefinite leave to remain. Paulette arrived in Britain in 1966. She had no need to apply for leave to remain. She was already here legally; it was the Home Office that was acting against the law. The letter, however, said that she was an illegal immigrant and had six months to leave the country. Her housing benefits were stopped. She became homeless. For two years she lived with a friend and depended on her daughter, Natalie, for financial support. She was the first nationally reported case of a scandal that would consume many others.

Anthony Bryan, like Paulette, legally came to Britain as a young child and was threatened with deportation as an adult.[5] He left Jamaica for Britain in 1965, when he was eight, to join his mother in London. He never returned to Jamaica; in fact he never went anywhere else. Britain was his home. For fifty-two years he lived and worked in the country as a painter and decorator, bringing up children and grandchildren, paying his taxes. Then, as a sixty-year-old man, he was told by the Home Office that he was an illegal immigrant and was requested to leave the country. A last-minute intervention from an immigration lawyer prevented his plane departing to Jamaica. Anthony had originally arrived in Britain on his older brother's passport. He received his initial letter from the Home Office in 2015 because he had applied for a passport for the first time in his life. He was informed that he had no right to remain in the UK, and that his employer would face a fine of £10,000 if it continued to employ him. He lost his job. He had never claimed benefits and had never opened a bank account; he struggled with filling out forms. In 2016 police and immigration officials arrived at his home with a battering ram and took him to the Verne immigration detention centre. They were going after a criminal – which Anthony clearly was not. With help from his lawyer, he was allowed to stay. But he should never have been threatened with deportation in the first place.

Another black Briton, Albert Thompson, was told that unless he produced a British passport he would be charged £54,000 for his cancer treatment.[6] In the summer of 2017 he was evicted from his home. He was homeless for three weeks. And he couldn't continue with his cancer treatment. He had paid taxes to Britain for more than thirty years. All of this didn't secure care and treatment for his dying body. Thankfully, though, he was given indefinite leave to remain in April 2018.

Many other cases emerged in 2017 and 2018. The British prime minister, Theresa May, apologised to twelve Caribbean heads of government in April 2018.[7] Amber Rudd, the home secretary, expressed deep regret and claimed that the Home Office did not have targets for removing illegal immigrants. But Lucy Moreton, the general secretary of the ISU, the union for immigration-service workers, claimed that Rudd was wrong: the Home Office did have targets.[8] Soon leaked letters were published by the *Guardian* revealing that in May 2017 Rudd had told Theresa May she wanted to increase deportations by 10 per cent. Rudd had misled Parliament. She soon resigned.

Paulette, Anthony and Albert all arrived in Britain in the 1960s to claim a status they were entitled to, as close relatives of people already in Britain legally. They were coming to the motherland. But some of their predecessors had even worse ordeals – ones that would foreshadow the brutal murder of Stephen Lawrence in Eltham.

* * *

Lord Kitchener, né Aldwyn Roberts, a Trinidadian singer, famously sang 'London is the place for me' for Pathé News upon arriving at Tilbury Docks in 1948 as part of the *Windrush* generation.[9] London was not the place for Kelso Cochrane. In May 1959 Cochrane, a carpenter from Antigua, was murdered on the streets of west London. He had moved to Britain in 1954, after a short stint in America. He was working as a carpenter in London to save up to study law; he never achieved this ambition. On the night of his death he was walking home from Paddington General Hospital after fracturing his thumb at work.[10] A gang of white youths saw him, followed him down the street and stabbed him with stiletto knives. When three other people came on the scene, the gang ran off. The three people took the wounded Cochrane to hospital; he died an hour later. It was Britain's first publicly acknowledged race-hate murder.

Many black people born in Britain, who have experienced no other country, have also been made to feel like strangers. This wasn't always through hostility. At times it was due to callous indifference. One of the most striking cases was the New Cross Fire of 1981. Yvonne Rudduck was having her sixteenth birthday party on 17 January 1981, in a house on New Cross Road, in south-east London.

That night Yvonne and twelve other young black people, most of them under sixteen, burned to death. Many others would be permanently injured. A raging fire had consumed the building. The police ruled out a racially motivated attack, and no one was ever charged with starting the fire. The queen didn't send a letter of condolence; the British government was indifferent to the tragedy. Orville and Eulalie Gooding, the parents of Andrew Gooding – one of the youngsters killed in the fire – received a letter in the post very soon after their fourteen-year-old son was burned to death. It said: 'It was a great day when all the niggers went up in smoke.'[11]

Sir David Lane, who was then the chairman of the Commission for Racial Equality, recognized that something was amiss between the British establishment and its increasingly ethnically diverse population. In a 1998 documentary interview on the history of black people in Britain, Lane was brutally frank about the response from many institutions in authority: 'I think it was a sign that our attitudes [to the New Cross Fire] – in the CRE [Commission for Racial Equality], in government, in Buckingham Palace – weren't fully on a wavelength with the multiracial community and didn't instinctively feel that the New Cross Fire is awful, [that] this is a national disaster... that we must take proper action.' There was also a fire in Ireland very soon after the New Cross Fire – and both the prime minister and the queen sent their condolences to its victims. The British establishment was willing to express compassion for a tragedy in a foreign country, but not to citizens in its own country.

Between 1945 and 1965 half a million people from the West Indies moved to the UK. The generation of Kelso Cochrane gave birth to the generation of Yvonne Rudduck and Stephen Lawrence; and brought along the generation of Paulette Wilson from the Caribbean to live with them in Britain. Cochrane's generation had a deep affinity with Britain, which they conceived of as the motherland, but they could always go back home to the Caribbean, and this was the plan for many of them: they saw their time in England as transitory. Ben Bousquet, the Labour Party activist who was born in St Lucia, expressed this view about how many West Indian immigrants viewed Britain:

> *I think what most West Indians who came to England in the fifties made of the England they came to was this: we've come here, we will work a while, we'll save some money and we'll go back home. It was just supposed to be a temporary gap, because we never came*

*here with any intention of doing any other
thing than to save some money, to educate our
children and to return home.*[12]

Paul Stephenson, the black British activist, said that most West Indians simply wanted to come, settle down, get their money and 'go home' – by which he meant back to the Caribbean island they came from. Sam Selvon's classic novel *The Lonely Londoners* captures the transitional nature of many West Indian immigrants. They came to the UK believing they were going to go back. The author George Lamming captures the strange experience of wanting to stay a short while in Britain, but staying for much longer than that, in his book *The Pleasures of Exile*, where he is writing about himself and his friend Sam Selvon:

*England lay before us, not a place, or a
people but as a promise and an expectation.
Sam and I had left for the same reasons.
We had come to England to be writers.
And now we were about to be anchored
at Southampton, we realized that we had
no return ticket. We had no experience
in crime. Moreover, our colonial status
condemned us fortunately to the rights of full
citizenship. In no circumstances could we*

qualify for deportation. There was no going
back. All the gaiety of reprieve which we
felt on our departure had now turned into
apprehension.[13]

Yvonne Rudduck's generation was born and
bred in Britain. This was their country; going back
was not feasible. This meant that any racism they
encountered stung all the more. They were being
alienated from their native homeland. This explained
what was at that time the largest black-led protest
in British history: in March 1981 there was a day of
action organized to protest against the negligence
and indifference of the British authorities towards
many of its black citizens. The march was from New
Cross to central London and 15,000 people took
part. Black British people had had enough. Their
sense of alienation from Britain had reached boiling
point. For many, Britain was not the mother country,
a place of paradisal comfort, to which they had a
strong affinity. It was a hellscape that condemned
them as outsiders.

The wave of immigration after the Second World
War was not the first time black people came to
Britain, but it was the first time the nation had a
substantial settlement of black people. Many of them
were literally returning. Around half of the people

on HMT *Empire Windrush*, for instance, had been living and working in Britain during the war by serving in the armed forces or in munitions factories. But they were coming home in another sense, too: all of them were officially British subjects carrying British passports – and from 1948 onwards they were Commonwealth citizens. Noel Brown, who served in the RAF during the Second World War and was a part of the *Windrush* generation, explained the affinity between the migrants and Britain in these terms: 'The King was our King. The flag was our flag. How much more British could we get?'[14]

The immigrants' attachment to Britain was often unconscious – it was completely internalized by many of them. Cy Grant, who came to Britain from Guyana and joined the RAF, was a handsome actor and singer who became the first black person to appear regularly on British television during his time at the *Tonight* programme (different from the BBC Radio 4 programme of the same name) in the 1950s and 1960s. He later claimed he never had a strong sense of British identity. This was because it was the *only* identity he ever really had: 'people from the Caribbean are not from the Caribbean originally. We were taken there, either slaves, or indentured labour, or whatever. And I didn't have any great strong feelings for Guyana.'[15]

Rosalind Howells, who served in the House of Lords from 1999 to 2019, was born in Grenada and moved to England when she was a child. She is similarly attached to Britain: she said the move was like going to a finishing school. And as a teenager, when people asked the author Colin Grant where he was from, he would say, 'British by birth but Jamaican by will and inclination.' If his Jamaican father, Bageye, ever overheard him saying this, he would berate the young Grant: 'Stop talk tripe. You born right here. You are English.' Grant adds that 'though Bageye never really expressed much enthusiasm for Britain, he had an uncomplicated attachment to his moral right to be here'.[16]

But the reality of Britain was shocking to many migrants. It undermined the perception some were accustomed to, from their education in the colonies: they thought white people were posh, but soon discovered that most of them were not. Stuart Hall, who arrived in Britain in 1950 as an undergraduate student to study at Oxford University, said this in a documentary interview about his first encounter of class in England: 'I'd never met ordinary, working English people. I'd met English school masters, English middle-class people, and colonial civil servants, and tourists and business people, but I'd never seen an English working man at home in an English pub with a London Cockney accent before.'[17] Many British people, meanwhile, were greatly ignorant about the Caribbean: some thought Trinidad and Barbados were places in Jamaica. When West Indian immigrants arrived, some of them were asked where they learned to speak English so well. Lenny Henry, the most successful black British comedian in history, recounts how his Jamaican mum came to Dudley, a town in the West Midlands, expecting a friendly welcome from the native citizens of the mother country; instead she was asked what part of Africa she came from.[18] It was a culture shock to both the immigrant and the native population.

Many white natives in England were not simply confused or ignorant, but openly hostile to this new wave of immigration. A *Daily Express* report on 21 June 1948 – the day before HMT *Empire Windrush* arrived – stated: 'Five hundred unwanted people, picked up by the trooper *Empire Windrush* after it had roamed the Caribbean, Mexican Gulf, and Atlantic for 27 days are hoping for a new life.'[19] In 1945 Clement Attlee's newly elected Labour government wanted the labour shortage in the country to be filled by European workers rather than black Caribbean people. The wrong sort of people were coming to the country. Many ministers in Attlee's government – the very same government that introduced the NHS and established the modern welfare state – were vocally anxious about black immigrants. On 8 June 1948 George Isaacs, the government minister of labour, said, 'The arrival of these substantial numbers of men under no organized arrangements is bound to result in difficulty and disappointment. I have no knowledge of their qualifications and capacity, and can give no assurance that they can be found suitable work.' Attlee wanted to divert HMT *Empire Windrush* to East Africa so that those on board could pick peanuts.[20]

The day the ship arrived, eleven Labour MPs sent a letter to their leader in which they argued that controls on black immigration should be put in place immediately. The British people, they wrote in that letter, are 'blessed by the absence of a colour racial problem', and 'an influx of coloured people domiciled here is likely to impair the harmony, strength and cohesion of our people and social life and cause discord and unhappiness among all concerned'. Ivor Cummings, an official in the Colonial Office, who was born to a Sierra Leonean father and a white British mother, told the people on the *Windrush* that things would not be easy for them. Tom Driberg, a left-wing Labour MP and later chair of the Labour Party, greeted some of the men staying in the Clapham bomb shelters and told them, 'Britain is not a paradise' and 'you have been warned that there may be difficulties caused through ignorance and prejudice, but don't let it get you down. Try and stand on your feet as soon as you can.'[21] Winston Churchill, who was re-elected as prime minister in 1951, thought in the 1950s that 'Keep Britain White' might make a good campaign slogan for a general election.[22]

But the immigrants had the law on their side. The British Nationality Act was passed on 30 July 1948, and it turned people living in the colonies from British subjects into Commonwealth citizens. As the historian Clair Wills notes, this was a ratification of an existing reality, in which members of the dominion and colonies were already entitled to citizenship.[23] The new Act was designed to enable those in the predominantly white dominions of the empire – Canada, New Zealand, Australia – to migrate back to Britain. But many of the people who came were immigrants from the Caribbean and South Asia: the countries of India and what was then known as West Pakistan (modern-day Pakistan) and East Pakistan (Bangladesh).

The Nationality Act came into force on 1 January 1949. However, the impact of this new legislation was only felt from the mid-1950s onwards. Between 1945 and 1950 the number of West Indians who moved to Britain was minuscule: just 5,000 people. From 1950 to 1954 it was still relatively small. Then it started to rise rapidly. Two events played a key role. In 1951 Jamaica was struck by Hurricane Charlie – the worst hurricane on the island since 1903. This made many Jamaicans want to leave to find better opportunities elsewhere. The other event was the introduction of the McCarran–Walter Act in America in 1952, which reduced immigration from the Caribbean to America. In 1955 immigration from the Caribbean went up by four times the rate of the previous year, from 10,000 to about 40,000. And in 1956, 46,000 migrants from the Caribbean came to Britain.[24]

By the early 1960s immigration to Britain had decreased. The fallout from the Notting Hill riots of 1958 convinced the government of Harold Macmillan that immigration restriction was a priority. The 1962 Commonwealth Immigration Act introduced a vouchers system. From now on, immigrants tended to be family members of people already residing in Britain or those with a job offer. This encouraged many of those who were already in Britain to settle down. Home secretary Rab Butler advocated for the immigration voucher scheme in the 1962 Immigration Act, which organized immigrants into three categories. As he put it in a letter:

The great merit of this scheme is that it can be presented as making no distinction on grounds of race or colour, although in practice all would-be immigrants from the old Commonwealth would almost certainly be able to obtain authority to enter under either category (a) or category (b). We must recognize that, although the scheme purports to relate solely to employment and to be non-discriminatory, its aim is primarily social and its restrictive effect is intended to, and would in fact, operate on coloured people almost exclusively.[25]

In 1965 Harold Wilson's government introduced further legislation that curtailed immigration. But this was accompanied by legislation that banned discrimination in public places and introduced a Race Relations Board, with the aim of conciliation and racial harmony. In 1967, however, the Confederation of British Industry and the Trades Union Congress compiled a joint statement that tried to oppose the Race Relations Act being extended to employment.

Kenyan Asians who held British passports, for instance, were exempt from the restrictions of the British Nationality Act 1965: they were still allowed to come to Britain as a matter of right. The 1968

Commonwealth Immigrants Act then got rid of the right of Kenyan Asians to migrate to Britain. In the *Spectator* Auberon Waugh, the conservative writer and critic, described it as 'one of the most immoral pieces of legislation to have emerged from any British Parliament'.[26]

In 1964 race also became a major factor in a British election for the first time in history. The slogan that supported Peter Griffiths in the Smethwick election was this: 'If you want a nigger neighbour, vote Labour.' The National Front was formed in 1966 (the group later rose in the 1970s; and in August 1977 the NF staged a demonstration against 'black crime' in Lewisham: 4,000 police officers escorted the Front through the area; their shouting slogan was 'Repatriation yes; immigration no!'). In 1968 Enoch Powell gave his 'Rivers of Blood' speech, in which he prophesied a race war unless immigration was drastically reduced, and emphasized that even the children of immigrants were fundamentally foreigners and would not assimilate in Britain. The leader of the Conservative Party, Ted Heath, sacked Powell from his Shadow Cabinet. More than three-quarters of the British public, however, backed Powell's speech, and hundreds of London dockers marched to Parliament to show their support for him.[27] Powell received more than 50,000 letters of support for his speech. Margaret Thatcher, who became prime minister eleven years later, said this about Powell's sacking, 'I thought it was a conclusion [that was] jumped to far too rapidly, if you look at the logic and reason in his speech.'[28]

Despite this painful history, to define black British life in the decades after the Second World War simply in terms of racist hostility is to undermine a rich variety of experiences. We shouldn't lose sight of the problems black people encountered; but we also shouldn't define them exclusively through those problems. They led complicated lives; there is more to the historical experience of being black and British than being a victim of racial prejudice. In these early years, though there was casual and institutional racism, there was also kindness from white British people. Sam King, who was born in Jamaica, and later became the mayor of Southwark in south London, stated, 'I would say a third of the people in Britain still had imperialist ideas. People from the colonies should be planting bananas and chocolate and whatever it is. Another third, I would say, did not really matter as long as Arsenal win on Saturday. The other third, they were just nice, ordinary people.'[29]

Black British people stuck out and many of them felt they needed to be more engaged in politics. In the 1980s there was a move to have greater representation for black people: the Black Sections movement was founded by black members of the Labour Party to try and implement this vision. Labour was the party of the black Caribbean population of the UK. When the demand for Black Sections was placed before the Labour Party conference, however, it was rejected. The scheme for greater racial representation, according to the authorities, illustrated racial separatism and left-wing extremism. This was the decade of concerns about the 'loony left'; the wilderness years of the Labour Party, with Trotskyist infiltration of Liverpool councils; and a manifesto in the 1983 general election that was described by the Labour MP Gerald Kaufman as 'the longest suicide note in history'. But the Black Sections did ultimately achieve some success. In the 1987 general election, Britain elected its first three black Members of Parliament: Paul Boateng, Bernie Grant and Diane Abbott. Representation had finally arrived.[30]

It was not only in politics that black people became part of the furniture of British society. With John Barnes in football, Soul II Soul in music and Lenny Henry in television, black people cemented their status as inextricably British. And even if they didn't do things as prominently as those names, or with great distinction, they should still be entitled to be treated with an equal level of dignity as their white counterparts. It was on the basis of their Britishness that the claim against racial prejudice was most pointedly made. If Stephen Lawrence had been a Brazilian immigrant to London, his murder would still have been obscene, but it was that sense of denied Britishness that made it particularly painful, and that so stung Paulette Wilson and the other victims of the *Windrush* scandal. Being attacked by family is a greater tragedy than being attacked by strangers. In her interview with the *Guardian* journalist Amelia Gentleman, Wilson was asked whether the designation of her as an illegal immigrant had made her question her national identity. 'I don't feel British,' Paulette responded to Gentleman. 'I am British. I've been raised here, all I know is Britain. What the hell can I call myself except British? I'm still angry that I have to prove it. I feel angry that I have to go through this.'[31]

Her passion recalls the patriotic affirmation of James Baldwin: that an identity is something that is a matter of fact, rather than a conjecture that needs to be proved. But the difference between Baldwin and Wilson is also crucial: she was doing it in a British context. The anger of many people, both black and white, towards the *Windrush* scandal only makes sense precisely because we already accept that people like Paulette are British.

You can't understand the travesty faced by Paulette without understanding Britain. Nor can you understand the pain of Ngozi Fulani without understanding how immigration is crucial to comprehending black British identity. In America the black population is not an immigrant group; the question of 'Where you really from?' or deportation would simply not carry the same resonance as it does in Britain. Post-war immigration to America has largely come from Hispanic and Asian people (and a small number of Africans). Britain, by contrast, has a black population where the overwhelming majority are either immigrants or the children of immigrants. We should never forget these differences. But sometimes we do.

Paulette Wilson died in June 2020 before she was given her full compensation. I was too distracted by the din of the Black Lives Matter protests to notice her death. Many of the victims of the scandal have still not received their full compensation. Some of Stephen Lawrence's killers were convicted in 2012, but it shouldn't have taken nearly twenty years for justice to arrive. The case of Ngozi Fulani and Lady Susan Hussey gained prominent media publicity, but the full implications were not clearly defined: that a black woman who identified so strongly with an African identity emphasized her British identity as being indivisible; and the royal family – an institution associated with the British establishment – so quickly acceded to this fact and punished Hussey for questioning it. Black British people are a part of Britain; this affinity is sometimes made invisible by the tragic reality of racism. But it nevertheless remains true. And any form of anti-racist politics needs to insist on it.

5

EMPIRE

Who is the greatest British person of all time? William Shakespeare? Charles Darwin? Charles Dickens? Queen Victoria? David Beckham? Queen Elizabeth II? Paddington Bear? In 2002 the BBC tried to find out. It commissioned a poll in which it asked the British public to cast their vote. More than 30,000 people voted by telephone or email. A list of ten names was soon drawn up. After the poll, BBC Two made a series of ten programmes, hosted by the formidable Anne Robinson of *The Weakest Link* fame, in which a guest was invited to defend his or her preferred choice for the greatest Briton of all time. After all the programmes were aired, there was a second poll. This time 1.6 million British people voted and, with more than 400,000 votes, there was a clear and convincing winner: Sir Winston Churchill.[1]

In February 2021, almost twenty years after the BBC first commissioned the poll that commemorated Churchill as the greatest British person of all time, there was a panel discussion at the University of Cambridge in a college named after the iconic British statesman. The discussion at Churchill College was entitled 'The Racial Consequences of Mr Churchill'.[2] It sought to demythologize the central image that we have of him: the indefatigable hero who saved Britain from fascist tyranny. Instead the panel situated Churchill in the context of race and empire. They came to a clear conclusion that went against the BBC poll. Churchill was not worthy of veneration; he was a white supremacist and an imperialist.

Battles over the legacy of the British Empire are one of the most vexed areas of the race debate in Britain today. The British Empire has played an important part in the formation of black British identities. America, too, was once a British colony, but as I have mentioned before, its black population does not comprise immigrant communities; and they do not come from a country that either currently has the British monarch as head of state or did within the past seventy years. Along with the topic of immigration, any discussion about black people in Britain needs to reckon specifically with the consequences of British colonialism. The Sri Lankan-born writer and resident of Britain A. V. Sivanandan famously said: 'we are here because you were there'.[3]

This debate speaks to questions of truth and myth, belonging and marginalization. Many people argue that the British public is in denial about the noxious legacy of the British Empire, and that this explains much of the racism that pervades British society. Unless this is confronted, they add, Britain's ethnic minorities will continue to be marginalized. This is a powerful argument. But it is incomplete in some parts, and mistaken in others. This issue should be approached with greater sensitivity rather than broad brushes; it is more complex than a morality tale.

During the George Floyd protests in the summer of 2020, Churchill's statue in Parliament Square was vandalized by red spray paint.[4] Those who morally object to Churchill would argue along these lines: he was a racist imperialist who had little sympathy for the working classes. He was responsible for the Bengal famine that led to the death of three million Indians during the Second World War. He described Indians as 'a beastly people with a beastly religion'. He called Mahatma Gandhi a 'malignant subversive fanatic'.[5]

Leo Amery, the secretary of state for India during the Second World War and a contemporary of Churchill's at Harrow College, wrote that on the topic of India he didn't 'see much difference between

[Churchill's] outlook and Hitler's'. Churchill, as I mentioned in the previous chapter, said 'Keep Britain White' would make a good campaign slogan for the Conservative Party in a 1950s election. He was also offensive about Chinese people: 'I hate people with slit eyes and pigtails. I don't like the look of them or the smell of them – but I suppose it does no great harm to have a look at them.' He was a passionate defender of the British Empire, and his conception of empire was paternalistic: he thought the Anglo-Saxon race had a duty to look after the supposedly backward races within it.

Professor Kehinde Andrews attacked Churchill's legacy when he debated with Piers Morgan on ITV's breakfast show *Good Morning Britain* in 2020, and in the Cambridge discussion panel he described Churchill as 'the perfect embodiment of white supremacy'. According to Andrews, the links between Churchill and the evils of colonialism are explicit. They simply can't be brushed aside. What is more, they show that Britain's values are not characterized by fairness and equality: they are underpinned by oppression. If Churchill is a hero to the nation, this shows that Britain is a racist and colonialist country that has failed to reckon with its past.

There have certainly been brutally violent episodes in Britain's colonial past and they deserve to be widely known. In the 1950s the British colonial government in Kenya launched a campaign of terror, castration, forced labour and torture against the native Kikuyu people.[6] They called it Operation Progress. More than a million Kenyans were forced into concentration camps to be re-educated and civilized out of their rebellion against British dominance. As part of the colonial policy, the British government got rid of troves of files that they stored in a facility the Foreign Office shared with British intelligence agencies. It was a mass cover-up. In 2009 the Harvard historian Caroline Elkins acted as the first expert witness for some of the suspected Mau Mau rebels to sue the British state over its use of torture and violence against them. Her 2005 book, *Imperial Reckoning*, which won the Pulitzer Prize for General Nonfiction, served as the basis for this claim. The case was called *Mutua and Others v. the Foreign and Commonwealth Office*. The claimants, who numbered more than 5,000 victims, eventually won in 2013, and David Cameron's government offered an official apology, £20 million and a monument to commemorate the victims, which was placed in Nairobi's Uhuru Park.[7]

In her later book, *Legacy of Violence* (2022), Elkins broadens her case against the British Empire beyond Kenya. She investigates events such as the Indian Mutiny (1857), the Morant Bay rebellion in Jamaica (1865), the Irish War of Independence (1919–21) and the post-Second World War states of emergency in Malaya and Cyprus. She writes in meticulous detail about 'corporal punishments, deportations, detentions without trial, forced migrations, killings, sexual assaults, tortures, and accompanying psychological terror, humiliation and loss'.[8] These acts of colonial violence were justified under a civilizing mission: the British wanted to shepherd 'backward' peoples into the modern world. 'Violence was not just the British Empire's midwife,' Elkins argues, 'it was endemic to the structures and systems of British rule. It was not just an occasional means to liberal imperialism's ends: it was the means and an end for as long as the British Empire remained alive.' The British Empire envisioned itself as a liberal enterprise, and violence and terror were integral to implementing this vision.

The major criticism of our colonial past is that it is defined by amnesia and pride. We either celebrate colonialism as a noble endeavour or we forget the bloodshed we unleashed. In *Legacy of Violence*, Elkins quotes from a 2014 survey, which found that almost 60 per cent of people in Britain think the British Empire is something to be proud of.[9] In his 2021 book, *Imperial Nostalgia*, the writer and historian Peter Mitchell argues that a sentimental attachment to the British Empire shapes contemporary British debates over race, class, gender and Brexit. Kojo Koram, a senior lecturer in law at Birkbeck University, expressed a similar sentiment in his 2022 book *Uncommon Wealth: Britain and the Aftermath of Empire*. He argues that Britain has continued to have an exploitative financial relationship with the countries it once colonized, even after these countries have gained independence.[10] Those who point out that Britain abolished the slave trade in 1807 and slavery in 1833, these writers argue, whitewash the brutality of slavery by casting the nation in an unjustifiably benign light. Britain should never have practised slavery in the first place. As the influential Trinidadian historian and politician Eric Williams once put it: 'British historians wrote almost as if Britain had introduced Negro slavery solely for the satisfaction of abolishing it.'[11] There is a consensus amongst this group of historians and thinkers: the British Empire was an ultimately deplorable endeavour, and its legacy continues to haunt contemporary Britain.

For many critics of colonialism, it was the Enlightenment – the intellectual movement in the seventeenth and eighteenth centuries that advocated for reason over superstition, and liberty over despotism – that laid the groundwork for the scientific racism and violence that characterized the British Empire. According to Kehinde Andrews, the Enlightenment was not animated by the principle of human equality. It was a form of white-identity politics; it provided intellectual justification for enslaving Africans and committing genocide against indigenous Americans. Many Enlightenment thinkers expressed racist beliefs.[12] The Scottish philosopher David Hume wrote: 'I am apt to suspect the negroes and in general all other species of men (for there are four or five different kinds) to be naturally inferior to the whites.' The German philosopher Immanuel Kant, who conceived the most memorable motto of the Enlightenment, *sapere aude* (Latin for 'dare to know'), also thought white people were superior to other races. He argued that 'humanity has its greatest degree of perfection in the white race' and that 'the Negroes are much lower'.

Voltaire, the embodiment of French Enlightenment thought, believed that a different racial group constituted a different species; he was also an anti-Semite. Thomas Jefferson, the main author of America's Declaration of Independence, a key Enlightenment-period text, affirmed that he 'never yet could find that a black has uttered a thought above the level of plain narration'. He also owned more than 600 slaves in his lifetime. G. W. F. Hegel, perhaps the most acclaimed German philosopher in the first half of the nineteenth century, argued that black Africans were a 'race of children that remain immersed in a state of naiveté'. And John Stuart Mill, arguably the most influential liberal thinker of all time, thought that Indians were backward and it was the job of the British to civilize them. Even Karl Marx argued that empire was a historical necessity rather than a moral abomination: 'England,' he wrote, 'has to fulfil a double mission in India: one destructive, the other regenerating – the annihilation of old Asiatic society, and the laying the material foundations of Western society in Asia.'[13]

As it happens, it is not only post-colonial theorists and historians of empire who advance a critique of the Enlightenment. John Gray, the political philosopher, has argued in his 2007 book *Black Mass* that there is a strain within the Enlightenment that had its origins in Christian millennialism (the idea that evil can be overcome in the world and that we can perfect humanity).[14] The inevitable outcome of this utopian ideology is violent terror. Gray argues that the Jacobins of the French Revolution first embodied this ideal, and it was later expressed through the great totalitarian ideologies of the twentieth century: Soviet communism and Nazi Germany. For Gray, writing in the mid-2000s, the contemporary incarnation of the ideology was American's War on Terror, and the attempt to transform countries like Iraq and Afghanistan into liberal democracies through the use of military force. Gray believes that politics should be a way of coping with human imperfection rather than trying to overcome it; we can't force countries to adopt the norms that give rise to liberal democracy overnight. He didn't write about British colonialism in his book, but one could synthesize his arguments with the one expressed by Elkins: that the British Empire acted savagely because of, rather than in spite of, its mission to impose progressive values on the rest of the world.

Much of this criticism of the Enlightenment is true. But it is not the full truth. The German philosopher Walter Benjamin once said that 'there is no document of civilization that was also not a document of barbarism'.[15] But Elkins's account in her most recent book only gives us the barbarism. We don't get the other side. In terms of the Enlightenment itself, for example, it was not just one single movement. It was riven with tensions. The historian Jonathan Israel, for instance, distinguishes between a radical Enlightenment tradition (epitomized by the Dutch Jewish philosopher Spinoza) that emphasized a universal humanity, and a moderate version that accommodates the existing inequalities in society.[16]

Imperialism, too, was not one singular ideology committed to suppressing native communities in Africa, Asia and the Caribbean. It had other dimensions. As the Oxford historian John Darwin argues in his *Times Literary Supplement* review of Elkins's book: 'We cannot defend or deny the atrocities visited by the British on those they saw as their enemies, or the racist assumptions that enabled the sometimes contemptuous attitude to non-European life. It is right that these should be recorded and exposed.'[17] Nevertheless, the British Empire was more than a record of atrocities. Darwin adds that it 'engaged with colonial peoples in many ways other than by violence: religiously, educationally, architecturally, philosophically, medically, scientifically and through ideas about law and – perhaps surprisingly – justice. Much of this has survived. Even as we reject the morality of colonialism, it is too reductionist to see its legacy as simply or mainly one of violence.'

The Christian missionaries are one instance of a benign form of colonialism. Chinua Achebe's novel *Things Fall Apart* is partly about the decline of pagan religion and the ascendancy of Christianity in southern Nigeria, and this is reflected by the conflict between the protagonist Okonkwo and his son Nwoye (Isaac).[18] The missionaries, more than the colonial government, established schools and discouraged practices hitherto common in pre-colonial Nigeria – human sacrifice, slavery, twin infanticide and polygamy. Christian missionary schools also provided the foundation for many forms of African nationalism. Pro-independence leaders, such as Obafemi Awolowo and Nnamdi Azikiwe, were educated at schools established by Christian missionaries. Ghana's Kwame Nkrumah was educated at a Catholic missionary school.[19] If practices like human sacrifice were wrong, these activists affirmed, then so too was colonial domination. Paradoxically, it was a feature of colonialism – the gradual expansion of literacy, and exposure to some of the ideas in Europe – that ultimately fuelled resistance to the practice of it. It also made a nonsense of the argument that Africans are naturally stupid and should thus be ruled by a white elite.

Black people are not stupid; they can govern themselves. This is a tenet of liberalism. Although liberalism could justify the use of terror and oppression, it could also provide liberation. The historian and writer Sunil Khilnani, in his excellent review of Elkins's book for *The New Yorker*, argues that it is too simplistic to define liberalism merely as a fig to justify domination.[20] He writes that 'Just as the nature of colonial governance varied across time and space, so did liberalism, whose "perfidiousness" is as much a bête noire of Elkins's book as empire is.' He adds that 'strains of liberalism embraced or accommodated paternalism, racism, and authoritarianism, helping provide intellectual cover for unimaginable cruelty.' But liberalism had another side: 'liberal philosophies also elaborated ideas of autonomy, individuality, and collective self-rule that, in turn, seeded principles about legitimacy that anti-colonial thinkers and activists enlisted to their cause.'

Khilnani's review is useful in thinking about Kehinde Andrews's patronising attitude towards Africans. For Andrews, Africans are almost always passive. When he writes about Rwanda, for example, he argues that 'the unspeakable horror of Rwanda was entirely a production of western imperialism'.[21] Entirely? The actions of Belgian colonial authorities certainly played a role in fostering ethnic tensions between the Hutus and the Tutsis. But to say they are 'entirely' responsible for the genocide is a gross oversimplification. What happened to human agency? Furthermore, his denunciation of the West betrays quite how Western he is as a thinker. In one instance, he bemoans the injustices caused by 'the Enlightenment and its universalist philosophy'. But in another telling passage, when he is describing the inequalities between Western nations and the Global South, he writes that 'the fact that $4 a day is labelled "working middle-class" should be proof of the obscenity of this paradigm. Conditions that we would never accept in the West are marked as progress in the Rest.' He is upset that we don't judge the Global South by the same standard we use to judge the West. He also believes that 'the only solution to the problem of racism' is by uniting 'Africa and the African diaspora' to 'create a true revolution'. This hasn't been done because 'a group of countries, including Nigeria, and most of Francophone Africa, were fundamentally opposed to truly unifying Africa. Instead they sought the trappings of nation-state sovereignty and maintaining close links to their paymasters in Europe.'[22] In other words, a continuation of divide-and-conquer has been encouraged by post-colonial African leaders who are in cahoots with Europe and America. The irony in this is that the notion of African unity, or Pan-Africanism, as I mentioned in an earlier chapter, was created by black people who were influenced by universalist ideas that derived from Europe.

C. L. R. James, the Trinidadian Marxist intellectual and hero of black radical thought, was a partisan of Enlightenment values. He didn't see the Enlightenment as an oppressive ideology, but as the opposite. His book *The Black Jacobins* is, among other things, an argument that the slave rebellion in Haiti advanced the principles of the French Revolution: equality, liberty and fraternity. Unlike Andrews, James was fully cognizant of where his ideas came from. He recognized many of the moral shortcomings of European empires, but he also proclaimed, 'I didn't learn literature from the mango tree, or bathing on the shore and getting the sun of colonial countries; I set out to master the literature, philosophy and ideas of Western civilization. That is where I have come from and I would not pretend to be anything else.'[23]

The British Empire was not morally straightforward. This is why we need a more nuanced account of its legacy. One attempt at this is an influential recent book on the relationship between modern Britain and the British Empire: Sathnam Sanghera's book *Empireland*. Sanghera argues that we can't understand modern Britain without understanding the British Empire.[24] From the food we eat to the immigrants in our society, from the language we use to the particular type of racism we practise, all of this can be traced back to the nature of our empire. This has significant cultural and political ramifications. Sanghera suggests that Brexit, for instance, occurred in large part because of empire – one of the reasons

Britain chose to leave the European Union is because we have not come to terms with the fact that we are no longer the metropole of a large empire, and the desire for free-trade agreements around the world is an attempt to revive our imperial ambitions.

However, there are some issues with Sanghera's argument. As the journalist Stephen Bush put it, in a joint review of Sanghera's book and Andrews's *The New Age of Empire*, countries such as the Netherlands and France are key parts of the EU and are unlikely to leave soon, but they haven't come to terms with their imperial legacies, either: in fact, racism is a pressing issue in both countries.[25] Moreover, multiple studies, including one by the British Social Attitudes Survey in 2017, have found that Brexit was motivated by a desire to be more inward-looking rather than expansionist: less immigration, less globalization.[26] People wanted to leave the EU not to revive imperial ambitions, but in recognition of the fact that such ambitions are permanently lodged in the past and Britain must now focus more on its own turf. One way to think about this is to consider again the life of Enoch Powell. He was an imperialist who proudly served in the Indian Army, learned Urdu and, as health minister, went to Barbados to recruit more nurses for the NHS. But Powell soon recognized that the British Empire was finished, ended up as an anti-imperialist nationalist, campaigned against joining the EU and suggested that black and Asian people should be repatriated in his infamous 'Rivers of Blood' speech.[27] The link between imperialism and racism is not straightforward; in many instances racism is motivated by nationalism, not imperialism, and the two things are not identical.

Many of the historians who condemn British exceptionalism replicate it by focusing almost exclusively on the evils of Britain, without comparing it to other continental countries. A survey compiled by the European Agency for Fundamental Rights entitled 'Being Black in the EU – Second European Union Minorities and Discrimination Survey' found that Britain was amongst the countries where the population had the least hatred against people of African descent.[28] Britain is one of the most tolerant countries in Europe on matters of race. The survey also showed that many of the countries that have never been colonizers, but have often been colonized – such as certain nations of Eastern Europe – have native populations with the most racist attitudes. Paradoxically, it seems that many countries that used to have empires are more tolerant *precisely* because they have greater familiarity with the wider world. (To use a very different example, and to mention again the ironies of imperialism, some twentieth-century Jewish writers like Joseph Roth had a nostalgia for the Austro-Hungarian Empire because it offered a far greater degree of protection to minority communities than the various nation-states that followed the dissolution of the empire.[29])

* * *

Sanghera's book was published in 2021, and the previous year saw many of the conversations about empire burst spectacularly into the open. On 7 June of that year, at the height of the George Floyd protests in Britain, a statue of a man, which had stood in central Bristol for 125 years, was broken from its plinth and thrown into Bristol harbour. Edward Colston, who was born in 1636 and died in 1721, was a pivotal figure in the British slave trade. He was a board member and later deputy governor of the Royal African Company. He was responsible for the trafficking of more than 80,000 slaves from Africa to the New World. Nearly 20,000 of these slaves died en route, their exhausted and disease-ridden bodies being dumped into the Atlantic Ocean. They were never remembered or commemorated. But Colston was. Now it was Colston's statue, put up in late-Victorian England at a time of imperial pomp, that was tossed into the water.[30]

The black Americans the Reverend Al Sharpton and the rapper Ice Cube both expressed support for the toppling of the statue. David Olusoga, the acclaimed British historian and author of *Black and British*, defended the action in a piece for the *Guardian* the very next day: 'Whatever is said over the next few days,' he wrote, 'this was not an attack on history. This is history.' For him, the action was an act of resistance from Bristol's ethnic-minority population against a white establishment that had tried to suppress the brutal history of Edward Colston. Olusoga wrote, of the people who defended the presence of the statue, 'They were confident that black people and brown people who call Bristol their home would forever tolerate living under the shadow of a man who traded in human flesh, that the power to decide whether Colston stood or fell lay in their hands.'[31] Curiously, though, the four people charged with removing and dumping the statue were all white: Sage Willoughby, Rhian Graham, Milo Ponsford and Jake Skuse. Olusoga spoke as an expert witness in their defence during their trial in Bristol Crown Court in December 2021. In 2020 Boris Johnson proposed ten-year sentences for anyone who defaced monuments. The Colston Four, as they became known, were expected to be convicted in court. But all of them were acquitted.[32]

Most British people in fact wanted the statue to be brought down. It was a question of how it was done. According to a YouGov poll in 2020, the majority of the British public supported the statue being dismantled: 53 per cent.[33] But of that number, only 13 per cent supported the statue being brought down in the way it actually was – torn from its plinth and dumped in Bristol harbour. What do black British people think? According to the poll, 31 per cent of black British people supported the statue being brought down *and* the way it was done. Many black people agree with Olusoga's point of view. But many others don't: 34 per cent of black British people supported the statue being dismantled, but disagreed with the way it was done. More black British people take the moderate position on this issue rather than the radical one. There is no homogenous black voice on such contentious issues. David Olusoga does not speak for black Britain, nor should he be expected to. He speaks only for himself.

The British public is also increasingly comfortable talking about race and identity, and adopts more nuanced positions than it is given credit for, by those who either condemn or defend the British Empire on stark moral grounds. According to a poll commissioned by the think tank Global Future in 2022, which was conducted by YouGov, three-quarters of the British public are comfortable talking about race and identity.[34] The idea that the British people are in denial about the evils of empire is also untrue. Although 77 per cent believe Britain has been a force for good in the world, 67 per cent also believe it has done some damage in the world. On racism, the public is likewise more sensitive to racial injustice than it is typically given credit for, by those who are understandably animated by this topic. Two-thirds of British people, for example, think that racism is one of the factors that explains disparities between racial groups.

The British public is not in denial about racism and empire: we simply think of it in more nuanced terms than is generally supposed. We love our country and we love our heroes; but we are not blind to the evils our country has perpetrated. Nuance, for those who think any position but radical indignation implies complicity with racism, is lost in the loud din of the culture wars. According to an Ipsos Mori poll conducted in June 2020, a month after George Floyd was murdered, more than 80 per cent of the British public supported peaceful protests in favour of greater racial equality and justice; 80 per cent disapproved of Donald Trump's aggressive response to the protests and demonstrations.[35] The issue is not whether racial justice is right or wrong, but the nature of such protests; 90 per cent of British people don't think violent protests constitute an appropriate response to a police officer killing an unarmed man. Colston was an evil man; his statue should have been brought down. Racial injustice is intolerable. But we can't get rid of it through the use of violence or vandalism. The latter goes against the spirit of British people – including black British people. This is not an earth-shattering answer. But social justice can't rely on exciting answers if it cares about what people think rather than what they ought to think.

* * *

There is another element about empire that makes it such a divisive issue: in valorizing imperialists, so the argument goes, we risk marginalizing the contribution of black British people and other ethnic-minority people to the British story. In the BBC poll of 100 greatest Britons ever, for example, there was only one person of colour: the singer of the band *Queen*, Freddie Mercury, who was of Parsi Indian ancestry. In response to this, Patrick Vernon and Angelina Osborne ran a separate poll to find the 100 greatest black Britons. In February 2004 a winner was announced: Mary Seacole. She was the

Jamaican-born nurse who helped British and French soldiers during the Crimean War of the 1850s.[36]

In 2020, in response to the *Windrush* scandal and the Black Lives Matter protests, Vernon and Osborne decided to establish another list, and it wasn't based on a public vote. This time it was published in the form of a book. David Lammy described it as 'an empowering read' and said, 'it is refreshing to see someone celebrate the role black Britons have played in this island's long and complicated history'. It was also praised by the Labour MP Dawn Butler and by the mayor of London, Sadiq Khan. David Olusoga wrote the foreword to the book and said, 'We share a national fascination with our colourful past, but one colour has been largely missing: Black. The history of Black people is unique in how comprehensively and consistently it has not only been overlooked but denied.'[37] The problem is that this book is as guilty of this charge as anything else. It makes some strange omissions and some odd inclusions. It complains about a mythologized past that consistently excludes black people; but it is committed to its own set of myths, where people from the past who were not black are included, at the expense of black people who have made valuable contributions to British society.

Sir Trevor Phillips, for instance, is not on the list.

Phillips was head of the EHRC (Equality and Human Rights Commission) in Britain, and a godfather of modern race relations in this country. He was also the executive producer of an influential documentary on the *Windrush* generation, which was aired in 1998 to commemorate the fiftieth anniversary of the *Empire Windrush* landing. This documentary won multiple television awards and revived interest in the history of black lives in Britain. It has influenced, among other things, Andrea Levy's acclaimed 2004 novel *Small Island*. But Phillips has criticized aspects of multiculturalism and contemporary identity politics, and I suspect this was one of the reasons he was omitted.

John Barnes, the England and Liverpool star, was the best footballer in England in the late 1980s and was playing for the best club at the time. He was the victim of vile racial abuse from opposition fans, including, as one famous image shows, banana skins being thrown onto the pitch. He was likely omitted because of his contentious views on race: one example that springs to mind was his defence of the actor Liam Neeson, after Neeson confessed to having violent racist fantasies in the past. What makes the omission strange is that football plays an important part in the lives of many black British people.

Zadie Smith has been the most well-known black British literary novelist for more than twenty years. When I was thirteen and knew next to nothing about contemporary literature, I knew who she was. Perhaps Smith was omitted because she has been a longtime resident of America? This makes no sense: the actor David Oyelowo, a longtime resident of California, is on the list. Oyelowo has been living in America and playing American characters for so long now that he joked in an interview with *The Times* that when playing British characters he almost needs a dialect coach. And yet Zadie Smith's name is not on this list. She has also written critically about identity politics in literature. Or maybe they simply forgot to include her. And forgot to include Phillips and Barnes. Or simply thought their contribution to British society was insufficient. However, Trevor Phillips, John Barnes and Zadie Smith *were* all on the list. If they were not excluded in 2020 on the basis of ideological differences, then it must be because of sheer incompetence.

I write this not because I think these figures should be entitled to feature in such a pantheon, but because Vernon and Osborne included two queens of England – Philippa of Hainault and Queen Charlotte – who were not, by any contemporary or historical standards, black. They were included simply on the rumoured speculation that they were black. Remarkably, the book by Vernon and Osborne also lists, as one of the criteria for inclusion, 'To have used their platform, privilege or status to support the advancement of the Black British community while being a British resident and/or citizen'.[38] Queen Charlotte and Queen Philippa clearly did not do this. And neither, for that matter, did Mary Seacole, the person voted Britain's greatest-ever black Briton in 2004. That criterion is nonsense in any case. There is no such thing as a single black British community. Being a great black British person should not mean that you have advanced the interests of black British people; it should only mean that you have done or achieved great things while being black and British. The intellectual confusion on display in this book illustrates the lack of sophistication by many people who engage in discussions about race and representation. They don't think through these issues with enough rigour. Many of the people involved in this project also make themselves vulnerable to the charge of hypocrisy: if we take their uncompromising stand against the British Empire, for example, then the likes of Patrick Vernon and David Olusoga should not have accepted their OBEs. The award stands for Order of the British Empire.

In order to emphasize the connection between black lives and Britain, history has assumed a great significance. As the previous chapter shows, you can't understand black people in contemporary Britain without understanding the particular history of black people on this island. But history is not something fixed in stone; it is contested. Nevertheless, this search for black heroes should not degenerate into the kind of pious myth-making that many progressive historians condemn some British people for engaging in when they glorify the British Empire. The search for heroes must be balanced by a respect for the truth. And a respect for the truth must also accept that the truth is often complicated. This is illustrated by the complex views of the British public. What the British public think would be of little relevance, if the argument is not that British society is in denial about imperialism; but that is often the claim, so we must attend to the issue.

On Churchill, for example, the picture is now more complex than at the time of the 2002 poll. We don't universally worship Churchill. A 2022 poll by the think tank Policy Exchange found that only one in five British people between the ages of eighteen and twenty-four has a positive view of Churchill.[39] It also found that 58 per cent of over-sixty-fives view him positively; 36 per cent of the British public overall view the wartime leader in a positive light. That is just one poll. Another YouGov poll from 2022 is more positive for Churchillians, but not perfect. It finds that 76 per cent of baby-boomers have a positive view of him compared to 55 per cent of millennials. There is a generational divide here. According to the more recent 2022 Policy Exchange poll, 17 per cent of eighteen- to twenty-four-year-olds think the British Empire did more good than harm; it is 61 per cent for the over-sixty-fives. There is so much more going on in these debates than the simplification that British society is deluded or in denial about empire and racism.

We should not mythologize Churchill; but we should accept that he took a vital stand against German fascism at a time when this was necessary. Clement Attlee, arguably Labour's most influential leader ever, described Churchill as 'the greatest leader in war this country has ever known'.[40] Denis Healey, former defence secretary and chancellor of the exchequer for the Labour Party, wrote in his memoir *The Time of My Life* that 'Churchill had defects on the same scale as his virtues. But his virtues made up for a lot.'[41] Trying to highlight Churchill's moral shortcomings is valuable; trying to definitively condemn him is a fool's errand that shows a contempt for the nuanced views of most British people – black or white. In order to reflect truthfully the legacy of the British Empire, we need to be more grounded in our approach and to resist the lure of morally dogmatic positions.

6

DISCRIMINATION AND DISPARITIES

Imagine a young British man called Tyler. He is black Caribbean. His grandparents came to Britain from Jamaica in the early 1960s. Both his parents were born in Britain. Tyler struggled through school. He did not go to university or attend a vocational course. Entering adulthood, he found it hard to get a job. He soon got involved in petty crime and was punished severely by the criminal justice system. There are too many Tylers in British society.

Now imagine a young British man called Taiwo. His parents migrated to Britain from Nigeria. He achieved exceptional grades at school, got into Cambridge University to study history, completed a law conversion course afterwards and is now a trainee solicitor at a prestigious law firm in the City of London. Although we often hear about Tylers, we don't hear that much about Taiwos. But the Taiwos are just as much a part of the black British experience as the Tylers.

A clear understanding of racial disparities in Britain today is an important part of a grounded approach to countering racism. But to what extent are racial disparities – the fact that some black people do worse in employment, education, the criminal justice system and other areas of civic life – a consequence of racism? This debate is hotly contested and can often degenerate into abusive slanging matches. The media often presents one side as denying the existence of racism and the other as race-grifters. We should approach the evidence of racial discrimination with greater care. But we should also acknowledge that there is more to British life than statistical data. In certain instances, such as in employment and parts of the criminal justice system, racism explains some of the racial disparities. But if we genuinely care about inequality, we shouldn't assume that all racial and ethnic disparities are because of racism. To do this would be to commit the disparity fallacy (explored in an earlier chapter through Coleman Hughes and Bayard Rustin). This is not because racism doesn't matter or doesn't exist. It is because racism is not the only thing that defines inequalities in our society. Inequalities might arise because of other factors, such as gender, geography and cultural attitudes to education. One of the great dividing lines in Britain is class. If racism is the only crucial factor in explaining disparities, then only Tylers would exist. There would be no Taiwos. This is not the case.

One book that came out in May 2017 tried to explain what causes racial disparities: Reni Eddo-Lodge's *Why I'm No Longer Talking to White People About Race*. And before we get to the content of that book, it is worth reflecting on its impact across wider society. The success of writers like Eddo-Lodge has reignited the question of representation in professions like the arts and publishing. She has also transformed the nature of the race debate in Britain. Her book was a *Sunday Times* bestseller. It won the Jhalak Prize in 2018. It was the winner of the Non-Fiction Narrative prize at the British Book Awards. It was Foyles' Non-Fiction Book of the Year and Blackwell's Non-Fiction Book of the Year. It was long-listed for the Baillie Gifford Prize for Non-Fiction and for the Orwell Prize for Political Writing. The acclaimed Jamaican novelist Marlon James described Eddo-Lodge's book as 'essential' and 'begging to be written'. Its cover was instantly iconic: the words *to white people* in the title are blanked out, while the rest of the title is in striking black. The website gal-dem described it as 'the black British Bible'. The title is deliberately provocative and ironic; its success relied on white people reading it and engaging with its content. Many celebrities and social-media influencers singled the book out as a key text in understanding racism after George Floyd's murder in America. In June 2020 Eddo-Lodge became the first black British woman to top the UK non-fiction paperback list compiled by Nielsen BookScan.[1]

I am myself a direct beneficiary of this increased interest in books about race. I welcome this debate. But I think the problem with the debate is that it is too insular. Natalie Jerome, a black British literary agent, wrote a column for the *Guardian* in which she said that she was sent a list 'of the top editors working across the major publishing houses in the UK. When I read it I burst into tears. It showed a sea of almost totally white faces.'[2] She mentions research commissioned by two large publishing firms, Penguin Random House and Hachette, which found that only 2.7 per cent of their staff members are black. She doesn't mention that black people constitute about 4 per cent of the British population. 'In a modern, multicultural nation,' she writes, 'the whiteness of the industry matters.' But she doesn't make the case for why publishing is a great industry for black people in the first place. The industry does not pay well and does not offer great job security. And most of the industry is based in a city with exorbitant house prices: London.

With all the discussion about improving representation, little thought is put into the perspective of black people themselves and their families and communities. Do many black people hanker for roles in publishing? Some obviously do. But if you are a talented child of ambitious but not well-off immigrants, for instance, why would you go into publishing rather than professions that pay much better, such as law, medicine or finance? This is a practical question. While representation can be important, anybody who wants to improve the lot of black British people should at least be curious about why they are better represented in some professions and under-represented in others. For example, in a country in which black people make up 4 per cent of the population, 6 per cent of junior doctors are now black.[3] Would the country – or black communities –really benefit if more black Britons chose to ditch medicine for a publishing internship? Would black parents be delighted if their children abandoned a career in finance to pursue a job in the arts sector?

This is not to condemn publishing and the arts as useless; these industries produce some of the things

I care about most passionately in my life. This is also not to argue that black people shouldn't pursue whatever industry they want: my dad wanted me to be a lawyer, but I have ended up as a writer (he seems happy with that decision now). What I am suggesting is that racial bias is not the only consideration when we are thinking about under-representation in industries. The debate is certainly worth having. But instead of a rigorous debate, there have largely been thoughtless paeans to diversity. Publishing companies are promising to be more diverse. What they should promise instead is to pay their workers a much better salary: this might encourage more ethnic-minority people to join.

The word 'class' is not mentioned once in Natalie Jerome's column. But class is critical to any discussion about representation in publishing and many other industries. Although at Penguin Random House only 2.7 per cent of the workforce are black, according to Jerome more than one-third of its staff were educated at a fee-paying school, something that applies to just 7 per cent of the British population. If you come from a well-off family, with a lot of intergenerational wealth, you can afford to pursue a career in publishing more than if you don't come from such a family.[4] This is not to say everyone in publishing comes from a wealthy background; this is clearly not the case. It is to point out that the structural incentives favour families with a great degree of wealth. Black people generally don't come from such families. This should be taken into account in any discussion on diversity in the arts. The stereotype of the West African parent who wants their child to study law or medicine is rooted in reality; the view that what publishing needs is more black faces (without addressing some of the class-related reasons that explain why they don't join) is a pointless diversion.

Another issue is the diversity of books being published by the industry. Are the demands of readers of colour being met? This is difficult to tell definitively because there is no foolproof way of measuring it. If we look at large-scale bookshops like Waterstones, they often have sections dedicated to black writers and Asian writers now. I am writing this chapter during Black History Month, and the Amazon website has a recommended list of books by black writers. There is an emerging list of black British writers whose titles have been critically and commercially successful: Caleb Azumah Nelson, Bolu Babalola, Candice Carty-Williams and many more. Yomi Adegoke's 2023 novel *The List* was bought by the publishing company 4th Estate after an eleven-way auction.[5] But why should we assume that black readers only want to read books by black writers or featuring black characters? And why should we assume that reading fiction and non-fiction books on race necessarily makes one more enlightened on the issue? It might, but it might not. Such things should be taken on a case-by-case basis. Representation without considering the complex interests of black people does not materially improve our lot or make white people more knowledgeable about us; it is simply window-dressing. This is not good enough.

* * *

The problem of relying too much on race to explain aspects of society is also evident in Eddo-Lodge's book. Her argument is not about individual or interpersonal acts of racism. Her focus is on structural racism. 'We tell ourselves,' she writes, 'that good people can't be racist. We seem to think true racism only exists in the hearts of evil people. We tell ourselves racism is about moral values, when instead it is about the survival strategy of systemic power.'[6] Whether or not you are personally prejudiced against someone from a different racial background is not the issue at hand, when it comes to understanding racism. What really counts is recognizing the systems and institutions that disadvantage black and other ethnic-minority people: 'this [argument] isn't about good and bad people'. It is about power.

According to Eddo-Lodge, racial power explains the racial disparities in society. Something is racist if it hinders one group of people at the expense of another. The British education system is structurally racist because black students do poorly at school compared to white students. The same is true, she adds, of employment and the criminal justice system. Black and other ethnic minorities are less likely to be employed; they are more likely to be imprisoned. We also shouldn't view these institutions in isolation. They interact to harm the life chances of black people in Britain. 'It seems like black people,' she writes, 'face a disadvantage at every significant step in their lives.'[7] If a black kid doesn't do well at school, this decreases his chances of getting a good and stable job, or any kind of job. This in turn increases his chances of getting involved in criminal activity – and he is eventually punished by a punitive justice system full of affluent white people who have no conception of, or sympathy with, his dysfunctional education and impoverished plight. On this basis, Britain is a structurally racist society. This network of institutional discrimination – in education, employment and criminal justice – combines to undermine the prospects of a good life for a black person. He is shafted by the British system. This explains the life of Tyler.

It's understandable why Eddo-Lodge believes this. Historically, many black students were disadvantaged in schools: teachers undervalued their academic abilities by wrongly consigning many of them to overcrowded and underfunded special educational schools. Many white teachers thought black kids were rowdy and uninterested in school. Confidence was seen as boastfulness; quietness was seen as idiocy.[8] In terms of criminal justice, black men have often been demonized as savages prowling the streets, and the police have made insufficient efforts to protect black communities from attacks by racist criminals. In terms of housing, meanwhile, black families have been overcharged in the past for grossly substandard accommodation by exploitative landlords. These are the facts. Eddo-Lodge's message resonates with many black British people because they recognize, from historical understanding and their own personal experiences, that while Britain has often preached tolerance and equality, the reality has at times been hatred and prejudice.

Some recent reports also seem to back up the conclusions that Eddo-Lodge arrives at in her book. According to the *Guardian*, a Runnymede Trust report from 2022 found that 'Black and minority ethnic people in the UK are more than twice as likely as white people to experience "deep poverty" – extreme levels of hardship meaning they struggle to afford everyday basics such as food and energy.' As the reporter Patrick Butler puts it: 'despite making up 15% of the UK population, minority ethnic people account for 26% of those in deep poverty. They were 2.2 times more likely to be in deep poverty than white people.' Another recent report has concluded that the British judiciary is institutionally racist. As the journalist Haroon Siddique writes:

> *The judiciary in England and Wales is 'institutionally racist', with more than half of legal professionals surveyed claiming to have witnessed a judge acting in a racially biassed way, according to a report. The study by the University of Manchester and barrister Keir Monteith KC found judicial discrimination to be directed particularly towards black court users – from lawyers to witnesses to defendants.*[9]

Siddique adds that 'The overwhelming majority (95%) of respondents said that racial bias played some role in the processes and/or outcomes of the justice system.' One survey by the Crest Advisory think tank in November 2022 found that only 46 per cent of black people trust the police.[10] This is compared to 64 per cent of white people. Amongst black Caribbean people, in particular, the figure that trusts the police is just 35 per cent. Another investigation from that same month, this time by the *Sunday Times*, found a culture of 'racism, sexism and bullying' in the Fire Department.[11]

On the basis of this, Reni Eddo-Lodge wants a radical solution to racism. The problem is that her account of what constitutes racism is too reductive. On the issue of education, for instance, it is simplistic to argue that white kids are doing better than black and ethnic-minority kids. Some white kids are doing better than some ethnic-minority kids. Some ethnic-minority kids are doing better than some white kids. In terms of GCSE and A-level attainment, for example, it has long been established that the highest-performing students in Britain are British-Indian and British-Chinese students.[12] In 2007 Bangladeshi students were 10 per cent less likely than white British students to obtain good maths and English GCSEs. Bangladeshi students are now 5 per cent more likely. If we focus simply on black kids, as Eddo-Lodge does, the picture is similarly complex. British-Nigerian students now do better than white British students in their GCSEs and A-levels.

Furthermore, if we look at progression to higher education, the picture is not so black and white. Only 40 per cent of white kids are in higher education by the age of nineteen compared to 62 per cent of black kids.[13] If we are focused on the very best universities in the UK (described as 'High Tariff' ones), black kids are doing better than white kids: they have a progression rate of 10.7 per cent compared to 10.5 per cent. In fact white students are the least likely ethnic group to progress to higher education, out of all the ethnic groups in the country: 65.7 per cent of South Asian kids and 81 per cent of Chinese kids progress to higher education. White British boys on free school meals have the worst outcomes in terms of progressing to higher education: only 13.6 per cent do so by nineteen. Meanwhile the share of the British population between nineteen and twenty-five that is BAME (black, Asian and minority ethnic) is 19 per cent. But 24.6 per cent of Oxford University's latest intake are BAME students. They also represent 25.4 per cent of the 2019 intake of Russell Group universities as a whole.[14]

On exclusion rates from school, the picture is also more complicated than the one Eddo-Lodge presents. Black African students are less likely to be temporarily excluded from school than white British students. The reason why black students are excluded more in general is because black Caribbeans are *three times as likely* to be temporarily excluded from school as black Africans.[15] If we look at permanent exclusion rates, the differences are similar. Black African students are less likely to be permanently excluded than white British students. One issue with Eddo-Lodge, and many others who imply that racial disparities are necessarily because of racism, is that they homogenize the experiences of black people. As the difference in exclusion rate shows, different black communities have significantly different experiences of the British education system. This is why we should not look at inequality in education through the lens of race: black African pupils are thriving; black Caribbean pupils are struggling.

Any analysis of race and ethnicity should thus not focus simply on the differences between white students and ethnic-minority students. It should also pay attention to the differences within races and ethnicities. Another significant difference between black Africans and black Caribbean students, for instance, is attainment level. Black African students have a higher educational attainment than their black Caribbean counterparts.[16] Many people, like the musician Akala, argue that such differences are because of class: black African kids do better because their parents tend to be better educated. In a 2018 interview with *VICE*, Akala said, 'It should be no surprise that immigrant kids whose parents were university-educated back home are doing better in school.'[17] But black Caribbean people are more likely to own property than black African people. If we look at another indicator of socio-economic background, free school meals, then black African kids on free school meals still do much better than black Caribbean kids on free school meals.

In terms of getting into university, these differences are still prominent. According to a report released by the Department of Education in July 2022, 53 per cent of black African boys on free school meals progressed to higher education by the age of nineteen in the year 2020–21.[18] The figure for black Caribbean boys, by contrast, was 25 per cent. The majority of black African boys on free school meals go to university. Only a quarter of black Caribbean boys do. Taiwo is more than twice as likely to go to university as Tyler.

If we focus on girls, the difference between black African and black Caribbean kids is still significant: 48 per cent of black Caribbean girls on free school meals, for example, progress to higher education. This is much better than black Caribbean boys, but the figure for black African girls is 69 per cent. And for those who are not eligible for free school meals, 80 per cent of black African girls progress to higher education compared to 60 per cent of black Caribbean girls. For boys it is 64 per cent of black African boys compared to 37 per cent of black Caribbean boys.

The facts with respect to education are significant, but all too often these distinctions are not taken into consideration. In terms of exclusion rates, for instance, the *Guardian* published a headline in September 2021 that stated: 'Black girls in England are twice as likely to be excluded from schools as white girls.'[19] It later amended the title to accurately reflect the finding of the report: black *Caribbean* girls (not black girls in general) are twice as likely to be excluded from school as white girls. Black African girls are in fact less likely to be excluded than white girls.

If we care about social justice, then specificity matters more than generalization. The point here isn't to deny that many black British pupils are doing poorly in education. Nor is it to say that racism plays no role in why some black students are doing badly. One could argue that the reason black Caribbeans are doing poorly is partly a legacy of racism: many black Caribbean kids were treated with such hostility and negligence by the educational system that they have a negative attitude to education, and this attitude was passed down to later generations. Black African students escaped this because their families moved to Britain at a later date.

There is nothing innately wrong with black Caribbean students. In fact in America they do very well in terms of education. Nevertheless, attributing these different outcomes solely to race obscures more than it illuminates: not all black British students are black Caribbeans, and the experiences of black Africans in terms of education are very different. Some black British communities are doing poorly, but others are doing extremely well. If we continue to conflate the experiences of black British students from different ethnic and cultural backgrounds, we can't have a targeted approach at improving the outcomes of the black students who are actually struggling. Disparities in terms of educational outcomes should take into account other factors, such as class, cultural differences, family formation and geography.

Curiously, however, Eddo-Lodge and many other writers and commentators who present a simplistic account of the relationship between education and race do not pay attention to all the other factors that might explain the disparities in educational outcomes. They argue that white people – simply by virtue of being white – have privilege; black people are underprivileged because of their race and little else. Therefore white students have an advantage over black and ethnic-minority students in education. This is not consistent with reality. If the education system were exclusively shaped towards advancing the interests of white people, this wouldn't explain why working-class boys do so badly while British-Indians and British-Chinese students do so well. Nor would it explain why the ethnic group with the worst educational outcomes comes from Roma/Traveller communities.[20] More to the point: this outlook doesn't recognize some of the unique difficulties faced by many poor working-class pupils of all racial backgrounds. Some of these difficulties include not just lack of funds, but also a lack of social capital: their families don't have the personal connections that wealthier families have, which can prove valuable in getting their child a job. There is also the lack of cultural capital: they don't possess the books and musical instruments at home that can nourish a child's knowledge and improve his or her chances at school. And there is insufficient attention paid to family breakdown and a family's attitude to education. A dysfunctional family is not conducive to a good education; neither is a family that is insufficiently focused on their child's education. The education researcher Feyisa Demie, in a 2007 report, for instance, links the great performance of black Africans in schools to 'strong parental support and links with African communities'.[21]

Geography also plays a key part in educational outcomes. As Chris Millward, the director for the group Fair Access and Participation, writes in a blog post: 'you need also to consider the influence of place. For white students who receive free school meals in London, the entry rate has pulled away from that in other parts of the country, and is now nearly eight percentage points higher than any other region. In London, less than half of the population is white, compared with 80 per cent across England as a whole.'[22] A major part of why some black and ethnic-minority communities are doing so well in education is because London is pulling away in education from the rest of Britain.

* * *

Once a black kid leaves school, how does he or she do? In terms of employment, there is some evidence of ethnic disparities regarding earnings. A report by the Institute for Fiscal Studies, which was commissioned by the Nuffield Foundation, finds that 'apparent educational success has not yet translated into better, or even equal, success when it comes to earnings'.[23] The median weekly earnings among employees for 'black Caribbean men were 13% below white British men in 2019'. This was also true of Pakistani and

Bangladeshi men compared to white men, as their pay was '22% and 42% lower, respectively'. But with Indian men their earnings were '13% higher than White British men'. One of the main insights of the report is that 'Indian men, both immigrant and UK born, have enjoyed rapid average wage growth. Black Caribbean men have not.' But the report also finds progress when it comes to employment rates amongst certain minority groups: 'Working-age Black African and Bangladeshi men had employment rates close to 30 percentage points lower than White men in the mid-1990s; by 2019, those same gaps were just 2–3 percentage points.'

Class is the key to understanding inequality in Britain when it comes to work. A pioneering study by the accounting organization KPMG published in December 2022, analysing more than 16,000 careers, found that social class is the biggest barrier to career progression in the UK.[24] It is a greater barrier than race or gender or any other diversity characteristic. If we look at some of the affluent professions, moreover, black people may be under-represented in the judiciary and among senior executives, but this is at least partly a consequence of a cohort effect. The black population skews younger, while the most senior positions in law and business are full of older people. Older people in Britain are more likely to be white. Still, in 2021 black people made up 2 per cent of lawyers in Britain, which roughly reflects the percentage of black people in the workforce (3 per cent). (The figure for ethnic-minority people working in law firms is 17 per cent, and they constitute around 15 per cent of the British population.) Black people are not under-represented in most areas of law.

What should be the threshold figure in order for an organization or a profession not to be racist? Forty-six per cent of all NHS doctors, for instance, come from an ethnic-minority background: ethnic minorities constitute around 15 per cent of the UK population; 31 per cent of senior doctors in the NHS come from an Asian background: Asian people constitute only 9 per cent of the UK population.[25] Employment disparities can occur because of racism, but they can occur because of other factors, too. We should not reflexively invoke racism. It's possible to simultaneously identify instances of racism in contemporary Britain and hold that racism does not fully explain the diverse experiences of black British people.

* * *

There might be some evidence of discrimination against black people in the criminal justice system.

Labour MP David Lammy was commissioned by David Cameron's Conservative government to investigate this. Lammy's report took eighteen months to complete and was finally published in September 2017.[26] He found that the proportion of ethnic-minority young offenders in custody had risen from 25 per cent in 2006 to 41 per cent in 2016; that the rate of black defendants pleading not guilty in the Crown Courts of England and Wales was 41 per cent between 2006 and 2014, and 31 per cent for white defendants; and that the proportion of ethnic-minority young people offending for the first time rose from 11 per cent in 2006 to 19 per cent a decade later. Summarizing his findings, Lammy said: 'My review clearly shows BAME individuals still face bias – including overt discrimination in parts of the justice system. It is only through delivering fairness, rebuilding trust, and sharing responsibility that we will build the equal and just society so often spoken about.' But Lammy is being simplistic in casting this as an issue affecting BAME people. It is affecting some black young men. He shouldn't infer widespread racial bias on this basis alone. In fact if we look at stop-and-search rates, black people are stopped and searched more than white British people, but British-Indian people are stopped at roughly the same level as white British people; British-Chinese people are stopped and searched at an even lower rate than white British people.[27] White British people are less likely to be arrested than black people. But Indian and Chinese people are less likely to be arrested by the police than white people. No one would argue on the basis of this that British-Indian people and British-Chinese people have 'privilege'. We need to be more specific in our focus.

We have established that some ethnic-minority groups are not disadvantaged in terms of education, employment and the criminal justice system. How can a definition of racism that affirms it is about prejudice and power account for racism against these particular ethnic minorities? We could say that these groups don't suffer from racism, but that would be nonsense and offensive. Or we could say some things that are true: racism doesn't come in one variety; disparities along ethnic lines don't necessarily illustrate the existence of racism; and some people manage to thrive despite the existence of racism.

* * *

Another problem with the definition of racism that is predicated on prejudice and power is that not only does it not account for the reality of ethnic groups who are not disadvantaged in education, employment and the criminal justice system. It also provides (unintended) justification for one of the oldest prejudices in Western civilization: anti-Semitism.

Many anti-racists invoke privilege to explain why some racial groups are doing better than others: they are doing better because they have a 'privilege' over other racial groups. This explains the concept of 'white privilege'. But anti-Semitism operates by casting Jewish people as privileged and exploitative of other races. This is why we need to be careful when we apply terms like 'privilege' to understanding racial disparities. If minorities who are successful – or are perceived to be successful – can only enjoy their success to the detriment of other minorities, then anti-Semites can view this reasoning as a vindication of their view that Jewish people are 'privileged'.

If racism is purely a result of prejudice and power, what language can we use to condemn black men from working-class backgrounds, for instance, promoting anti-Semitism? As the writer John-Paul Pagano puts it, 'when racism poses as resistance by victims of racism, as anti-Semitism often does, it disqualifies Jews from concern'.[28] There is the example of the British rapper Wiley. In July 2020 he used his Twitter account to promote the view that Jews were behind the transatlantic slave trade.[29] He also compared them to the Ku Klux Klan. For Wiley, there was an unavoidable tension between black people and Jewish people. 'Listen to me Jewish community Israel is not your country I'm sorry,' he tweeted. 'Israel is ours.' In his mind, he was exposing the exploitative role of Jewish music managers in contemporary Britain. Wiley genuinely believed that he was condemning structural power. Rather than recycling old anti-Semitic tropes, he was convinced he was fighting injustice. As the German social democrat August Bebel once said, anti-Semitism is the 'socialism of the fools'. Jews supposedly possess power and privilege; to call them out as such makes one a foe of structural inequalities. Wiley tried to present himself as a victim of a conspiracy led by Jewish managers against black musicians. Most people saw him for what he truly is: a vile crank.

In 2020 the American rapper Ice Cube shared on his social-media accounts an image of a group of hook-nosed men sitting around a table upheld by slaves.[30] The French comedian Dieudonné M'bala M'bala also constantly affirms that he is simply inveighing against the Establishment and Zionism.[31] And in December 2013, after scoring a goal for West Bromwich Albion against West Ham, the French footballer Nicolas Anelka performed a strange gesture with his arms: his right hand was pointed down and his left arm was across it. It looked like an inverted

Nazi salute. That was the point. The gesture is called 'the quenelle' and it was invented by Dieudonné. He believes Zionists (Jews) are behind much of the world's ills, and he presents his 'comedy' as a subversive force against this supposedly powerful foe. He has been convicted eight times of inciting hatred against Jews. And despite the fact that he typically invokes the language of social justice, he is an ally of Jean-Marie Le Pen, the former leader of the National Front party, who once said the Holocaust was 'just a detail in the history of World War II'; he was kicked out of his own party in 2015 by his daughter and successor as leader, Marine Le Pen, because his statements were too embarrassing to defend.

There is a vicious strain of anti-Semitism found in certain corners of black radical politics. Consider the Nation of Islam. This is the black nationalist organization that was founded in 1930, but which only gained prominence after the Second World War. The charismatic Malcolm X was the organization's chief spokesman. In 1991 the historical research department of the Nation of Islam published a book entitled *The Secret Relationship Between Blacks and Jews*, which argued that Jews were behind the transatlantic slave trade.[32] As part of his tirade, Wiley proudly shared his admiration for the Nation's leader, Louis Farrakhan, on the day of his Twitter rage.

According to this theory of anti-Semitism, Jews have stolen something that belongs to another group. They have assumed a status of victimhood at the expense of the true victims of society: black people. The actress and broadcaster Whoopi Goldberg said on the ABC show *The View* that the Holocaust wasn't about race: 'Let's be truthful, the Holocaust isn't about race, it's not. It's about man's inhumanity to man, that's what it's about. These are two groups of white people.'[33] Never mind that the Nazis regarded Jews as an evil race.

The musician Kanye West is another example of someone who thinks Jews have privilege.[34] In October 2022 he tweeted that he was going to go 'death con 3 on Jewish people'. He later stated in a podcast interview, 'I can say anti-Semitic things, and Adidas can't drop me. Now what? Now what?' Adidas dropped him. We need a multifaceted approach rather than a simplistic one.

We need to therefore discard the unsophisticated language of 'privilege' in favour of a more granular attention to the various ways in which prejudice can manifest itself. Although we have a shared British identity, and should thus be entitled to equal moral status, a useful form of anti-racist politics also needs to recognize that we are not all the same in terms of our racial, social, cultural, geographical and class backgrounds. And we should therefore be attentive to how these other factors can contribute to inequality. Digging deeper into these differences forms the next focus of this book.

7

BAME

In September 2021 six strangers from very different backgrounds arrive at a sumptuous mansion in the Cotswolds – a region in rural England that the novelist J. B. Priestley once called the 'the most English and the least spoiled of all our countrysides'[1] – to take part in a TV programme. One of them is a male doctor, another is a female security guard; one of them is a gay, young musician, while another is a straight and middle-aged professor; one of them is a property and litigation contractor, while another is a conservative political commentator. All six of them are British: three women and three men. And all six of them are black. For the next ten days, on a BBC documentary called *We Are Black and British*, they will discuss and reflect on what it is like to be both black *and* British – by discussing race and identity over dinner, visiting a school, observing a political rally and sitting together in a lounge-room.[2] What they find out should be obvious to anyone who has spent time talking to, listening to and living with black British people: they are not all the same.

Lin Mei is a thirty-four-year-old property and litigation contractor. Her father is black and her mother is Asian and white. Mista Strange, with his hair dyed blond, is a twenty-two-year-old gay rapper who grew up on a west London council estate. Michelle White is a thirty-six-year-old security guard and the single mum of two children. Kehinde Andrews (whom we've encountered before in this book, and will encounter again) is a thirty-eight-year-old university professor who established Britain's first-ever black-studies degree. Raphael Olaiya is a twenty-nine-year-old NHS doctor, the child of affluent Nigerian immigrants, and he grew up in Devon. Dominique Samuels, meanwhile, is a twenty-three-year-old political commentator from a working-class background in Manchester.

Their backgrounds are different, as are their beliefs. Dominique Samuels is a conservative. Dom, as she is called on the show, grew up in a single-parent household in a deprived part of Manchester called Moss Side. Her mum was looking after her and her sister with little help. Nevertheless, her mother was able eventually to create her own cleaning business, buy a house, move out of Moss Side and establish a new life with her two daughters: Dom was one of the few black girls at her new school. Her father was a drug addict who ended up killing himself, and Dom had a boyfriend who was stabbed to death. Her upbringing was chaotic and dysfunctional. There was a lot of trauma and pent-up fury. Unsurprisingly, she developed behavioural problems and was excluded from school after getting into a fight with another girl. She was devastated by her exclusion; she felt she had let her mum down. But unlike those who would argue that her exclusion was a consequence of systemic racism in British schools, Dom argues that what led to her exclusion was her own individual behaviour: she had wasted the sacrifice of her mother. Her mum worked hard to get her into another comprehensive, and Dom's attitude soon changed drastically. She became a straight-As student and demonstrated that you can achieve your ambitions simply through grit and determination. This is how she sees it anyway.

Kehinde Andrews, professor of Black Studies at Birmingham City University, sees it differently. He is not a conservative but a radical. He states that it is not the fault of the individual student if she is excluded from school. It's the fault of the system: 'all the evidence will tell you this is a systemic problem,' he states in the programme. 'This is a problem with the school.' The problems that black kids in Britain face do not exist in a vacuum. They derive from a social, cultural and historical context in which they are undervalued and demonized by a white elite. The only way to improve the lot of black people is through revolution – by upending this system rather than trying to reform it. This is because the system is rotten to the core. Teachers are institutionally biased against black students. They generally have lower expectations of black kids, and thus are more likely to punish them for minor transgressions than they are white kids. Dom's individual experience of success is only an exception to a norm: this is the argument of Kehinde.

Both Kehinde and Dom, despite these significant ideological differences, are black and British. Their beliefs have been informed by their particular experience of growing up in Britain. Kehinde often invokes the language of a black radical tradition that transcends national borders, but he does so with a thick Brummie accent: 'I'm black, I'm proud,' he says: 'Blackness is absolutely central to everything I do.' But he is a British citizen, and he has never lived anywhere else. He believes in independent black institutions to safeguard black people from racism. This is informed by his troubled upbringing. He went to school in a white neighbourhood and his school years were characterized by deep self-loathing. He desperately wanted to be white: 'I acted white. I had white friends. Even my musical taste was white.' He subscribes to the Black Panther motto: survival in this white supremacist society until we achieve the revolution. Kehinde affirms that black people need to survive the hostile systems in society by building up their own institutions and safe spaces. But this affirmation is hollow. Black British people constitute 4 per cent of the population in Britain. Building such institutions will not change the fact that we are a minority. The very need to build such institutions in the first place stems from the fact that we are a minority. It would be meaningless in a majority-black country.

These different backgrounds and beliefs often lead to heated debates in the programme. Such disputes should be welcomed rather than marginalized. A healthy civic society is one in which there is a plurality of views, and black British people should not be exempted from this: they are British people, and not all British people have the same social, cultural and political beliefs. Michelle is the only mother in the group, and her experience of being a mother to black children is similar to that of some other black women in this country. She gave birth to her first son when she was seventeen. And she was nineteen when she gave birth to her daughter. Michelle's son was once arrested by the police for carrying a knife that he needed for his job. The police officer later said that her son smelled of cannabis, something he categorically denied. Michelle says police hostility to black boys means she never sleeps until her son gets home from work. One would expect her to be hostile to the police.

Kehinde certainly is: he wouldn't want his kids to be police officers, and he wants to defund the police, get rid of police institutions and replace them with something else. He believes the only fair alternative to a police force that is institutionally hostile to black people is community policing. Black people should police themselves. But Michelle disagrees with this. Despite her experience, she is not hostile to the police: 'They're some bad, fucked-up police officers,' she says, but 'it doesn't mean that the whole system is bad'. Black British people may be the victims of racism, such as when they or their loved ones are unfairly targeted by the police or other figures of authority, but such terrible experiences do not imply that they want a radical solution to resolve this. Some do; many don't. Michelle's views are just as valid as those of any other black British person.

Lin Mei's story is the last one to be told in the programme, and it offers the most fascinating insights. Her mum is half Pakistani, half white English. Her father, however, is black and from Barbados, where he and Lin's mother met. Like an increasing number of black and British people, she is mixed-race: in fact mixed-race people are the fastest-growing (non-distinct) ethnic-minority group in the country. Lin Mei's experiences foreshadow those of the next generation of mixed-race British people. Her experiences of racism have been more complex as a consequence of her mixed heritage. She has experienced racist hostility from her mother's Asian side of the family, but she also feels pressure from certain elements of the 'black community': she's often asked, in other words, to pick a side: black or Asian. She doesn't want to fall into such tribal thinking. As a child, she was convinced she was black. She was born in a black-majority country – Barbados. But her mother told her she can't be black because to identify as such would be to deny her Asian heritage.

She's now a proudly mixed-race woman: 'If I say I'm black,' Lin Mei says in the programme, 'it's like eradicating half of me.' For her, the word black 'no longer serves a purpose'. She adds, however, that this is also true of the word 'white': 'Someone from Croatia is not going to have the same experience as someone from Scotland.' Lin Mei thinks we need to move beyond such rigid labels in order to reflect the complexity of each individual: what does being white or black *really* tell you about an individual person? She also thinks the category of black is all too often characterized by struggle: 'It pisses me off that our identity is based on struggle, when we're so much more than struggle.' Ultimately, for Lin Mei, black identity is often homogenized: 'we do not all think the same. And that is so refreshing.' This statement serves as a powerful summary of the programme, and whatever one thinks about her individual perspective, it provokes a more stimulating discussion on our attitude to racial categories.

* * *

Ethnic-minority people in Britain are very different from one another. The term BAME was always imperfect, but it is increasingly becoming of little use. There are important differences between racial and ethnic groups in Britain in terms of national background, religion, socio-economic outcomes and their attitudes towards each other. This is also true within racial groups; black British people are not all the same. This chapter argues that before we build a convincing picture of black British life, we need a more flexible approach to racial categories.

A 2014 report by Policy Exchange entitled *A Portrait of Modern Britain* illustrates the diversity of modern Britain. It states that 'clearly there is no single "BAME" community. Over 100 different languages are spoken on London's playgrounds alone.' And it adds, 'Families that came to the UK decades ago from the Caribbean will be quite different to recent arrivals from Somalia, or indeed Indian immigrants from East Africa. And single ethnic identities are themselves becoming more complex due to the growth of the Mixed population and generational change.'[3]

The report was written by two authors of South Asian descent. One of them is called Saratha Rajeswaran. The other author is Rishi Sunak, who was then the head of Policy Exchange's new Black and Minority Ethnic (BME) Research Unit. He was also a director of a company called Catamaran Ventures that was founded by his father-in-law. But in October 2022 he became Britain's first prime minister of Asian descent. When he was initially elected to Parliament in May 2015 he took his oath on the Bhagavad Gita, the most holy scripture for Hinduism. In 2020, when he was chancellor of the exchequer, he lit candles outside Number 11 Downing Street to celebrate the Hindu festival of Diwali: he called this one of the proudest moments of his political career. He became prime minister during the week of Diwali in 2022.

But Sunak's ascension is part of a general trend in the Conservative Party. Before Jeremy Hunt became chancellor in October 2022, the last four chancellors of the exchequer were called Kwasi, Nadhim, Rishi and Sajid; and Kemi Badenoch is touted as a future leader of the party. This is all in large part a consequence of the former Tory leader and prime minister David Cameron. As he put it in a *Sunday Times* column during the summer 2022 Tory leadership contest:

> *During my first week in the job, I made a speech explaining that it wasn't enough to open the door and say 'come on in' when all people would see was a sea of white male faces. We needed to get out there and bring people in. So I immediately froze the selection of Conservative candidates. I said that from our broader candidates' list we would draw up a priority list, of which half would be female and a large proportion would be from black and minority ethnic backgrounds.*[4]

But Sunak is more than simply an Asian person; that is not the only relevant aspect of his identity. He was educated at Winchester and Oxford, worked for Goldman Sachs and is married to the daughter of a billionaire. He comes from the south of England. His family also came to Britain through Africa, rather than Asia. This is another fascinating dimension to his identity. As Trevor Phillips writes of Sunak:

> *The third wave of Indian migrants turned up in Britain with virtually no possessions. But they brought a bucketload of what the social scientists might call social capital. In English this translates into a readiness to (in Sunak's famous phrase) do whatever it takes to succeed, eschewing short-term rewards for longer-term gains. And they have prospered, not only in politics but in business.*[5]

What characterizes this wave of immigrants is 'a profound belief in their own cultural uniqueness, strong impulse control and crucially an abiding sense of insecurity'. In other words, this wave of immigrants is distinct from other sources of immigration to Britain.

In May 2015 Phillips also gave a speech in which he described terms like BME and BAME as outdated. Such terms, he said, serve 'to tidy away the messy jumble of real human beings who share only one characteristic – that they don't have white skin'. The *Guardian* published a collection of responses to the speech.[6] Lola Okolosie, an author and journalist, described these labels as 'a necessity'. She added that 'they exist because society recognizes that discrimination is a fact which the law must acknowledge and seek to redress'. Ultimately, 'without these labels' we won't be able to know 'that certain people are far more likely to be stopped and searched on our streets or in our airports'. Still, Okolosie is uncomfortable with the labels: 'They are unwieldy and lack nuance. No one can deny that. My blackness is informed by whether or not I am Nigerian or Jamaican or half-white, poor or middle class. Blackness is not one thing, and it isn't experienced as such.' Her support for the labels and her discomfort with them are in direct tension. The label serves a political function, but it doesn't fully reflect reality.

Joseph Harker, a longtime editor at the *Guardian*'s comment pages and a former editor of the black British newspaper *The Voice*, had the following to say about Phillips's condemnation of the use of BAME: 'Here are four words I haven't used in a long time: Trevor Phillips is right.' Harker and Phillips have had many disagreements on issues of race. But on the issue of the term BAME, they are united. 'Because,' adds

Harker, 'more and more, the differences between our minority communities are growing – including how they are affected by racism – and so it's becoming increasingly unrealistic to package us all together.' Harker argues that there was a time when lumping all ethnic-minority people together was useful because of the common experience of racism. There was a time in the past when Asian people were considered black. The Southall Black Sisters, for instance, was an anti-racist organization created largely by women of South Asian descent. Peter Fryer's classic 1984 book about the history of black people in Britain, *Staying Power*, included the experiences of Asian people, too. But Harker thinks the differences between black and Asian people are such that the utility of such an umbrella term has expired. 'Over time,' he adds, 'the differences, such as religion and culture, became apparent and fed into the experiences these groups had in the UK. Black people integrated more into sport and entertainment', whereas 'Asian people had stronger family units, set up more small businesses, but tended to settle in areas, including northern towns, where there was more racial separation. In the late 1980s Asians started calling for a distinct, non-black identity. And then east Asians, who'd set roots here well before the *Windrush* arrived, began raising their voices too.'

Harker also looks at the difference in educational outcomes, which we examined in the previous chapter. He states that 'those of Indian or Chinese background are performing better in many areas than those originating from other parts of Asia; and Africans are outperforming Caribbeans. Indeed west Africans have very different experiences to east Africans in Britain.' He adds that that is before 'we even talk about those of dual or multiple racial backgrounds. But if we're all treated as BAME then an organization might fix a problem of Caribbean inequality, say, by appointing Indians. Diversity box ticked.' Yet the term BAME is still used by many institutions and companies today. Many of them have a noble intent: they want to improve the lives of non-white people in Britain; they want to fight racism. But they are doing so at the expense of those they are supposedly fighting in favour of.

Many British-Asian people also dislike the term BAME because they feel that their cultures and backgrounds are being marginalized. Nicole Miners, whose father is white English and whose mother is white Chinese, first heard of BAME when she was in drama school.[7] She told *BBC News* in 2020 that she hates it. 'Being a British East Asian actor, or just a person,' she said, 'this was something that really aggravated me.' One problem with it is that even the term 'Asian' is extremely broad: 'Does it mean "South Asian", "East Asian", "South East Asian", "Indian", "Pakistani", "Chinese", "Thai", "Vietnamese"? The list goes on.' What connects an Indian Hindu doctor to a Chinese atheist accountant or a Thai Buddhist cleaner, apart from not being white? Is being non-white an absence of something – sufficient to describe wildly divergent groups of people?

The British-Asian comedian Eshaan Akbar also dislikes the term. 'My experience as a British person who is half Bangladeshi and half Pakistani,' he said, 'is very different to a British black male or any other Asian.' The material concerns of one group of people do not always translate into those of another group of people: 'During the Black Lives Matter protests, "BAME" popped up yet again. But many Muslim Asians felt that issues happening in their community were being ignored.' He adds, 'the only thing I know we definitely have in common with other people in the "BAME" group is that we all have really good food.' The BBC, as part of their response to the Black Lives Matter protests, interviewed a twenty-year-old Nigerian student who first heard of BAME when she started university and discovered the existence of 'BAME officers'. These are students who are tasked with representing the interests of other ethnic-minority students at the university. 'I mean, it was a white term, if we're being honest,' she says. 'White people made it so they don't have to say "black", because they feel weird saying black for some reason.' She adds that 'I feel like "BAME" is just their safe word to not come off as racist.'

Many black and Asian people are not simply against the term; they also don't understand what it means. Zamila Bunglawala, a former deputy director of the Cabinet Office's Race Disparity Unit, wrote in a blog post that in a study of 300 ethnic-minority people, only a small number recognized the label BAME. Another problem she identifies with the term is that it fails to take into account the issues faced by white ethnic minorities in the country: 'There is also a problem in that the terms BAME and BME aren't always associated with white ethnic minorities such as Gypsy, Roma and Traveller of Irish Heritage groups, which we know are among some of our most marginalized and disadvantaged communities,' she said. 'To leave these communities out of the very language we use is to marginalize them even further.'[8] BAME is incoherent and confusing. It is not helpful.

Another reason why many black and ethnic-minority people do not like the term BAME is because of prejudices that exist between non-white peoples. In China, for example, many black visitors are often referred to as *hei gu*. This means 'black ghosts' or 'niggers'. In Bollywood, the Indian film industry, there is a widespread preference for lighter-skinned actresses. In Egypt and Sudan black people are often referred to by the Arabs as *Abd*, which means a slave.[9]

There has also been prejudice between different black communities. Many West Indians, for example, have been hostile to African communities. The Caribbean-born British activist Darcus Howe made a documentary for Channel 4 titled *Who You Callin' a Nigger* in 2004. In it, he documents clashes between West Indians and Somalis in south-east London. In a column for the *Guardian* about the documentary, Howe wrote:

> *I journeyed through Woolwich and Plumstead, where thousands of Somali refugees are settling. The Caribbean community is mostly unwelcoming. Some visit on Somalis the same kind of racial abuse we suffered in the period of early migration…* 'They are taking our houses. They are getting social benefits which are denied to us. Their children are overcrowding our schools.'[10]

One West Indian woman said this to Howe: 'I hate Somalis. They should go back to where they came from.' He noted that, as she said this, she 'did not bat an eyelid'. Why did Howe make such an inflammatory documentary? 'My detractors,' he wrote, 'will charge that such a documentary will strengthen the cause of the BNP... I reply to those who make the charge only that the programme represents the truth. Dirty linen needs airing. We have to be mercilessly realistic to make any assessment of who and where we are.'

There are other palpable differences between Africans and Caribbeans. Jeffrey Boakye is a black British author and schoolteacher. When his father moved to Britain in the 1970s from Ghana, he was shocked by the racism he encountered – not from whites, but from other black people. He was called a 'jungle man' and was mocked for his accent. He lacked the streetwise credibility of black Caribbean people. He was seen as 'fresh off the boat'.[11] Underpinning the prejudice against him was the sense that he was a foreigner in a way that a black Caribbean person, with an anglophone name and a longer presence in Britain, was not. As Jimi Famurewa puts it in his book *Settlers*: 'For a long time, to be "African" was many things. But – set against the culturally defining Blackness of, say, Bob Marley – it was never, ever cool.'[12]

Famurewa, like Boakye, was born in Britain to West African parents in the early 1980s. His family came

from Nigeria. In school Famurewa was ostracized
– not by white students, but by black Caribbean
students: 'It was a Jamaican girl in my Year 7 class,'
he writes, 'who first told me I was an African.' She
didn't mean it as a compliment. She said to him:
'You've got a proper big African nose, yuknow.' In
Famurewa's experience, 'some of the Caribbeans in
our orbit were introducing us to a whole new lexicon
of ridicule'.[13] Nels Abbey, an author and former
banker, was interviewed for Famurewa's book and
shares a similar experience to his: 'it just became
apparent that to be African was frowned upon. The
Jamaicans were the thing to be. And if you were not
Jamaican then you at least had to be from one of the
other islands like Barbados.'[14] Abbey, whose family
also arrived from Nigeria, started to claim a Barbados
identity so that he wouldn't be bullied at school by
the other black kids.

There is a historical dimension to these differences.
Many black Caribbean people came to Britain as
working-class labourers. Black Africans, meanwhile,
often came as students. Boakye comes from a black
African family. His upbringing was somewhat
different from that of the other black people he grew
up with in Brixton: 'I'm not Caribbean,' he writes
in his book *Black, Listed*, 'I'm African. Ghanaian.
With a whole other set of cultural norms shaping

my experiences in the home.' Some of these norms revolve around food and education: 'Days shaped around the preparation of traditional food to be eaten with fingers, church as a capital "E" event, being steered towards a university education at all costs, not being allowed to hang out on the estate with slow-moving rudeboys, perceived as a threat to success by paranoid parents.'[15]

Boakye seems to have also internalized the perception, when he was growing up in south London during the 1980s and 1990s, that being African was uncool. When he was a kid, the cool kind of black identity was the West Indian one: 'Youth culture,' he writes, 'hinged on West Indian, specifically Jamaican, cultural norms that have become ingrained in black British youth culture.'[16] The West Indian black person said *fuck you* to authority figures, smoked weed, possessed a charismatic dialect that evaded the understanding of the prim and proper; he was an urban folk hero. This was the blackness of reggae, ragga and dance-hall music. This was the blackness of Bob Marley. To be African, by contrast, was to be a nerd. The black African was a student, the Caribbean a street hustler; the African sucked up to authority, the Caribbean rebelled against it. The black African was a subject of mockery, while the black Caribbean was a subject of emulation: Matthew, the cringeworthy student in the popular British TV show *Desmond's*; Eddie Murphy's Prince Akeem in his movie *Coming to America*; and Nathaniel, the embarrassing Nigerian accountant played by the British comedian Felix Dexter on the show *The Real McCoy*.[17]

Of course this is a generalization. Many black Caribbean people, especially from older generations, share a similar attitude to education and authority to the later generations of immigrant black African families. And there are many black African figures, like the Nigerian musician Fela Kuti, who have led rebellious and decadent lives. But this perception still has a great degree of truth.

Boakye's family didn't want him to be a Jamaican, and the negative connotations they associated with that identity. They wanted him to be a good Ghanaian boy who would go to school, get good grades and make his family proud. It would have been worse for him if he were a girl: 'I distinctly remember elders in the Ghanaian community, aunties, uncles, instructing adolescent girls to not bring home a Jamaican boy under any circumstances.'[18] This illustrates, again, that there are different ways to be black and British. Is any one of them more authentic than the other?

* * *

The question of authenticity is not whether you are black or not black. It's a question of: Are you *really* black? Are you black enough? This question has often been filtered through an American cultural perspective. Boakye describes how, growing up, 'African-American cultural norms were being fed to us with unrelenting consistency, so much so that black America became a cornerstone of my identity as a black Briton.' This was the 1980s and 1990s, when musical genres like hip-hop, new jack swing and R&B were predominant, along with TV shows like *The Cosby Show* and *The Fresh Prince of Bel-Air*. They affirmed, in their different ways, an aspirational black identity. Those TV shows depicted what black middle-class respectability could look like; the music showed a thrilling form of black rebellion. 'For black people coming of age in pre-millennium Britain,' Boakye writes, 'America was a cool older sibling to look up to, or live vicariously through.'[19]

The coolness of black American culture is most vividly expressed through music. And this kind of music can generate a sense of belonging among black people across the world. In 1986 the black American band Cameo released a catchy song called 'Candy', and ever since there's been a particular type of dance associated with it. Boakye writes that 'if the first few notes of "Candy" by Cameo were to suddenly drift out of these pages and filter through the air, I'm certain that most, if not all, black readers would immediately drop the book, spring to their feet and get into formation for the Electric side'.[20] I am one of them. I remember first hearing the song as a child, and lost track of it as I got older. Then, during my first year of university, I rediscovered the song on Twitter, when a snippet of it was being played in a video. I needed to find the full song. When I did and played it on YouTube, it was like being reunited with a beloved lost family member, or being able to fully speak again a language you thought you had forgotten: my sense of completeness was overwhelming. It is now one of my favourite songs.

Music created by black people in America also finds resonance in Africa. Growing up in Nigeria, I felt a strong attachment to black American culture. I remember one day when I was little, and in my Nigerian home, watching the music video to Beyoncé's hit song 'Crazy in Love'.[21] I was with a babysitter, a girl in her late teens wearing red shorts and blue flip-flops. She was dancing along to Beyoncé's song, wiggling her hips, her face a picture of complete joy. Even today I can't recollect this memory without a wide grin. I danced along frantically too, a red lollipop in my mouth, moving with the gawky innocence of a seven-year-old. *She is one of us*, I thought then, watching the video and caught up in the experience: *Beyoncé is one of us.* I have cousins in South Africa who speak English with an American accent. When they were asked why they spoke like that, they said they grew up with hip-hop.

But it is not only black American music that can unite black people around the world. In 1999 a band from the Ivory Coast called Magic System released a track called '1er Gaou'.[22] If you look up the song's Wikipedia page, it looks like a fairly banal song by an African band, which had a decent reception when it was released in France in 2002. But I heard the song at practically every party or social function I attended when I was a small child in Nigeria. I was so familiar with it that I thought the lyrics of the song, which are an Ivorian-French patois, were from an obscure Nigerian language I couldn't understand. Up until this day, I don't fully know what the song is about; an online search suggests it's about a man with relationship issues. Nevertheless, I feel a powerful surge of pride whenever I hear it – and I would often go back to listen to it, to rekindle that feeling. Looking at the comments beneath the song on YouTube also reveals that it was played prominently in social gatherings in other African countries, from Ghana to Kenya and the Congo; it's also apparently popular in Haiti, too. Music can generate a cross-national sense of belonging. It can unite the global black diaspora.

The British philosopher Paul Gilroy argues in his 1993 book *The Black Atlantic: Modernity and Double Consciousness* that when it comes to culture, blackness can go beyond the nation-state.[23] According to Gilroy, there is a transatlantic black culture that connects America with Britain and Africa. He paid particular attention to music, and his argument is true today of musical genres like Afrobeats, which was first developed in West Africa, but is widely listened to in America and Britain. When the Nigerian Afrobeats musician Wizkid released tickets to his O2 Arena concert in 2021, they were sold out in twelve minutes.[24] Music and popular culture are borderless; we now live in a global village connected through the internet. I have a great fondness for, and affinity with, many pieces of African music that have a large audience in the Caribbean and North America – from Wizkid to Davido, from Rema to Burna Boy.

But appreciation for culture does not need to be racialized. I love black American culture because I love American culture in general. I liked hip-hop music; but I *adored* World Wrestling Entertainment and the action movies of Arnold Schwarzenegger. Many white people love Afrobeats and Wizkid. And hip-hop music wouldn't have been the huge commercial success it has been without the white teenagers in American suburbs who enjoyed it.

* * *

For Boakye, however, the 'key defining characteristic of the black experience' is not any type of cultural expression, like music, but the material reality of 'poverty'.[25] This is the source of black authenticity. This is the case because 'every black person I have ever spoken to has had some shared point of reference to an impoverished upbringing, probably because every black person I have ever spoken to was born in the twentieth century, and the twentieth century hasn't exactly been smooth sailing for the dark of skin'. Boakye even mentions the experiences of the successful black British journalist and author Afua Hirsch. She had an affluent upbringing, but she married a working-class black man. Boakye's arguments do not stand up to scrutiny. Many black people in the UK and the US live in poverty, but to define blackness in terms of poverty is both untrue and insulting. Hirsch's mother was the daughter of a Cambridge-educated Ghanaian diplomat. Is her mother any less black because of this? To go back to

Boakye, he himself is now a teacher and a successful author who speaks at the Hay Literary Festival. Does his current status dilute his black identity? If he genuinely thinks poverty is the 'defining' quality of being black, then surely it would.

Boakye writes that 'there's an inherent underdog quality to being black that acts as an ideological passport into black identity, something that not even wealth acquisition can remove. And nor do we want it to.' This sounds eerily like the American writer Norman Mailer's conception of black people in his essay 'The White Negro'. This is the black person as the eternal rebel, always struggling and hustling on the street. What underpins this fixation with an authentic black identity is Boakye's anxiety about being a sell-out. 'Out of all the labels in this book, Sellout is the one I want to avoid the most, which speaks volumes about the need black people have for black authenticity. For black people, the desire to be authentically, truly black is like thirst. It feels like sustenance.'[26] Being a sell-out means sacrificing your black identity. This is terrible because being 'black is such a heightened state of identity that it feels like it qualifies our existence. It defines us on a fundamental level, meaning that any rejection is a rejection of self. This is why I'm so paranoid about not being black enough.'

The word 'sell-out' is such a potent one that it has generated its own rich vocabulary of insults: Uncle Tom, Coon, Coconut, Aunt Jemima, House Negro, House Nigger. Boakye's anxiety about the term is reflected by the fact that he both thinks 'being a sellout is one of the most devastating things that can be levelled against a black person' and that 'I'm not sure if the concept really exists.'[27] What, exactly, counts as a sell-out? Some people think a black person is a sell-out if they support right-wing parties. The poet Benjamin Zephaniah once said that 'the strangest animal I've ever seen is a black Tory'. Black people who are critical of identity politics are also sometimes denounced online as coons. Marcus Garvey met the Ku Klux Klan, and Malcolm X met the American Nazi Party; both of these men, like white nationalist groups, were opposed to interracial marriage. Does this make them sell-outs? Or is being a sell-out someone who is happy to enter into romantic relationships with white people? James Baldwin was denounced as a sell-out by Eldridge Cleaver because Baldwin was gay, and Cleaver saw homosexuality as antithetical to authentic forms of black masculinity.

Boakye says that he has a white wife, white friends, enjoys cream-based pasta dishes and was never involved in petty crime. Yet, as if to assuage any discomfort about being a sell-out, he adds that he still likes hip-hop music and hot pepper sauce. I would maintain that if he didn't like those latter things he still wouldn't be a sell-out. But what do I know: my favourite novelists are Iris Murdoch and John Updike. 'Running in the background of the sellout conversation,' he writes, 'is a murmured debate surrounding class and social mobility. These pages are full of tensions surrounding identity and biography, one of the biggest being my transition from a black working class to a much whiter middle class form of identity.'[28] But this kind of thinking reinforces racial stereotypes rather than undermining them. He adds that 'it's the difference between being black as in what you are, and being Black as in who you are.'

Being black as in what you are, according to Boakye, means being poor; being black as in who you are means liking 'black culture'. So if you're a rich black person you can still cling to a black identity by liking Stormzy and thinking Michelle Obama is a goddess. Is Boakye scared that his newfound middle-class life – and the fact he was never part of the streets – means he has lost credibility as a black man? It seems he still wants to be part of the club; I would maintain he has never left any such 'black' club. Being middle or upper class and liking 'white culture' (an absurd phrase) doesn't disqualify someone from being black.

In fact I would maintain that codifying culture in racial terms runs against the guiding principle of anti-racism. The cultures of Europe do not belong exclusively to white people; they belong to black people, too. As W. E. B. Du Bois eloquently put it: 'I sit with Shakespeare and he winces not. Across the colour line, I move arm in arm with Balzac and Dumas. From out of the caves of evening that swing between strong-limbed earth and the tracery of the stars, I summon Aristotle and Aurelius and what soul I will, and they come all graciously with no scorn nor condescension.'[29] The novelist Saul Bellow once asked in the 1980s, 'Who is the Tolstoy of the Zulus?' To which a black American writer called Ralph Wiley responded twenty years later: 'Tolstoy is the Tolstoy of the Zulus, unless you find profit in fencing off universal properties of mankind into exclusive tribal ownership.'[30] Tolstoy belongs not only to Europe and North America; he also belongs to the Zulus. He belongs to all of us.

What also makes Boakye's argument confusing is that he is critical of 'white liberals' for many of the faults of which he himself is guilty, when it comes to black identity. He describes 'a generation of well-meaning liberals out there who are seeking something real in this Web 2.0 world, and what can be more real than the plight of a marginalized minority?' And who can blame these white progressives seeking something 'real' in the plight of a marginalized minority, and in fact seeing plight as the defining quality of this minority, when prominent members of this minority like Boakye think the very same thing? He complains that in the classrooms and playgrounds at his school he sees the relish 'with which black culture is consumed, but it stops short of real engagement with black history and heritages of black intellectualism'.[31] This is very much a 'blackness belongs to us rather than them' type of rhetoric. How many black kids, or for that matter black adults, are engaged with the 'heritages' of 'black intellectualism'? Most black kids are probably too busy focusing on their exams, or trying to get in the school sports team, or thinking about their crush. Most black people are not hung up on 'intellectualism'. This is not because they are black. It is because they are people; most people are not passionately engaged with intellectual matters.

Most black people are also secure in their identity; it's not something that can be defined *exclusively* in terms of particular qualities, such as poverty or nationality or religion or their tastes in music and food. It is just who they are. It is something that is lived. Trying to taxonomize blackness, as Boakye has done, is a wild goose chase. Blackness is not one single thing, and the fact of its multiplicity is a strength rather than a weakness.

* * *

The BBC programme *We Are Black and British* demonstrates that the term the 'black British community' is inadequate. There are black British *communities*. To be black and British alone cannot offer an *absolutely certain* guide as to a person's sexual preferences, whether they prefer Chinese to Indian food, their religious affiliation, their political affiliation, their political and social beliefs, the kind of work they do, the books or films or TV shows or music they enjoy, the country their parents or grandparents came from, the continent their parents or grandparents came from, the races of their parents, their irreducible sense of self. But black British people can't be understood in isolation; they can only properly be understood in relation to other British people. One way to think about this is by examining mixed-race British people: one of the fastest-growing ethnic-minority groups in the country.

8

MIXED RACE

Kwame Anthony Appiah is a racial chameleon. In São Paulo the natives think he is Brazilian and address him in Portuguese. South Africans consider him a Coloured person. Italians think he is Ethiopian. Some London taxi drivers speak to him in Hindi. In fact Appiah could trace his ancestry on his mother's side to a Norman knight who moved to Oxfordshire in the early thirteenth century. His father was an immigrant from Ghana. His mother, Peggy Cripps, was the daughter of Sir Stafford Cripps, a distinguished barrister and a chancellor of the exchequer under Clement Attlee's Labour government. Appiah's father, meanwhile, was Joe Appiah, a law student, anti-colonial activist, president of the West African Students' Union and President Kwame Nkrumah's representative in Britain. His parents met in England. His mum was working for an organization called Racial Unity that sought to promote racial harmony in Britain and the colonies, and this is how she met Appiah's dad.[1] As Appiah has often recounted, you could say that she put her principles into practice by marrying Joe Appiah. (Their marriage was an inspiration for the film *Guess Who's Coming to Dinner*, which starred Sidney Poitier.)

Appiah was born in London, brought up in Kumasi, Ghana, and in his grandmother's town of Minchinhampton, Gloucestershire, and educated at a boarding school in north Dorset called Bryanston and at Cambridge University. He currently resides in New York: one of the most cosmopolitan cities in the world. He is a brown-skinned resident of America who speaks English with a posh British accent. Appiah's personal history illustrates the extraordinary contingency of racial classification.

Black British identity is not fixed in stone. It is thus important to consider race and racial identity with care and rigour. One way to examine the fluidity of race is by looking at how mixed-race people are perceived throughout the world. In Western countries they are usually considered black. In many African countries, by contrast, they are thought of as basically white. Blackness is not a universal identity. It is shaped by national and local contexts.

The title of Appiah's 2018 book describes identity as 'the lies that bind'. In it he argues that 'too many of us remain captive to the perilous cartography of colour'. Identities matter a great deal to people. Appiah concedes this much. He writes that 'having an identity can give you a sense of how you fit into the social world'.[2] But even racial identities only tell a partial story. They don't offer the fullness of the individual. For that, we need to see identities in the round. Instead of defining someone simply in terms of their race and nothing else, we need also to consider how other factors such as nationality, language, religion, geography and class shape that person's racial identity.

Race is distinctive in America. There is a tension between the inherent fluidity of racial identity and the need to fix it into something binary. This tension has characterized American society for much of its history. Walter White was the leader of the most prominent civil-rights organization in America between 1929 and 1955: the NAACP. He had blond hair and blue eyes. His mum had the same features as him. All his siblings could pass as white. But the opening sentence of his autobiography is this: 'I am a Negro.'[3] Out of thirty-two of his ancestors, only five of them were black. In America, if one in thirty-two of your ancestors was black, you were officially black, under Jim Crow laws. In any other country in the world Walter White would have been considered a white man. But he was an American; so Walter White was black.

When I was growing up in Nigeria I had a neighbour called Paul. He was five years older than me, and I used to visit his house as often as I could because I found him so fascinating: he used to show me how to use his magnificent pair of binoculars, and I would often use them to stare out into our street, like a spy scoping out enemy territory in an action movie, or a humanoid eagle inspecting tiny people going about their daily business. It was tremendous fun. Paul was like a cousin or an older brother to me. But something else fascinated me about him. His dad was Nigerian and his mum was Russian. He had light-brown skin. It was darker than Walter White's skin. But to my eyes, Paul was not black.

The first nine years of my life were spent in Nigeria. It is the most populous country in Africa, and the country with the largest number of black people in the world. By the end of this century it is predicted to be the second most populous country in the world, behind only India; and the territory in West Africa between Abidjan in Ivory Coast and Lagos in Nigeria will be the most densely populated patch of land on Earth.[4] I grew up surrounded by black people. I thought I had an intuitive sense of what it meant to be black. My mum and dad were black. My brothers were black. Most of the people on the street were black. But my neighbour Paul wasn't black; he looked different from the black people I had seen every day. He had a lighter tint in his skin, which counted for everything. I also knew his mother came from a white country. To me, he was basically white.

Remi Adekoya, like Paul, grew up in Nigeria with a Nigerian father and a Slavic mother (his mum is from Poland). Adekoya is now an academic at York University. In his 2021 book *Biracial Britain*, he writes that in 'Nigeria, people don't look at me and see a black person'.[5] Instead, 'the Nigerian who hasn't had much contact with people of different races looks at me and sees an *oyinbo* (white person)'. For Adekoya, being mixed-race is shaped by where you are. 'When you are mixed race,' he writes, 'you are contrasted with the majority population of whatever society you are in.' Mixed-race people are considered black in the West because most people in the West are white. In African countries, however, they are often considered white. Our conception of what it means to be black emerges out of the social context in which we live. 'Blackness,' Adekoya writes in his book, 'has only really existed where there have been many white people, and black unity where there has been systematic white oppression.'[6]

Black people have their distinct cultural identities, which can't always be smoothly defined in terms of race: as Adekoya puts it: 'People who came here from Africa come with their own distinct ethnic identities, languages, and cultures, and don't see themselves as simply "black people". It is only in the eyes of others that they are seen that way.' This is true of someone like Chimamanda Ngozi Adichie, the acclaimed Nigerian novelist, who once said, 'I discovered I was black when I came to the US.'[7] In her native Nigeria, she is an Igbo woman. Almost everyone is black in Nigeria, but there are more than 300 tribes in the country and more than 500 different languages are spoken. Difference runs along the lines of culture and language and ethnicity and religion. It is not to be found in race. So when I said I thought Paul was white, what I meant was I thought he was different from me in a way I was not used to: different not in the sense of someone who came from a different ethnic group from me, like an Igbo or a Hausa person, or someone who came from a different religious background, like a Muslim, but different in a more alien way. He was a mixed-race person; I couldn't fit him in a box. So I *completely* othered him. I settled on thinking of him as white.

The question of mixed-race identity is especially important in a British context because 30 per cent of Britain's population will be mixed-race by the end of this century. Remi Adekoya's book *Biracial Britain* comprises a series of interviews with mixed-race people. One of them is a woman called Sophia. Her father came to Britain from Zimbabwe. Her mother is white British. 'Growing up' in the UK, she says, 'we didn't feel Zimbabwean. We felt black.'[8] The absence of a strong Zimbabwean community in Britain to which she could attach herself meant she ended up attaching herself to a general black identity. This identity was an antidote to the ostracization that she experienced from the majority white population. In particular, she embraced black American culture. She read the fiction of Toni Morrison; she read up on Malcolm X; her music tastes were black American musicians. She was a black woman, or at least she thought so. 'In Britain, I'm mainly a black woman. I've always felt black because that's how white people have treated me.' But in Zimbabwe, the reverse happened. After visiting Zimbabwe for the first time, as a young woman, she came to a stark conclusion: 'I'd never felt so white in my life.' To most people in Britain she was a light-skinned black girl, but to even her family in Zimbabwe she was white: 'It's weird when you grow up thinking of yourself as black only for people in Africa to see you as white. As not one of them. It's difficult to reconcile this in your head.'[9]

Daniela, another mixed-race woman that Adekoya interviews for the book, is a DJ whose dad is white British and whose mum is a black woman from Colombia. 'I'm not even white-passing in Britain, but in the eyes of my Colombian family I am basically white.' Even though she speaks perfect Spanish, and 'with a Colombian accent I learnt from my mum, Colombian taxi drivers still overcharge me. They can smell my foreignness.'[10] Being overcharged by the natives in another country is something Daniela shares with one of the most famous mixed-race people in the world: Barack Obama. He recounts in his memoir, *Dreams from My Father*, how his Kenyan sister used to insist on following him to the market because she was convinced he would be overcharged.[11] The market men were able to smell his foreignness, too. For Daniela, this was initially devastating for her sense of self. But being in a foreign land also reinforced her native sense of Britishness: 'I had built it up in my head that Colombia was where I could be me,' she says, 'but that trip actually taught me a lot about Britain and myself; how open Britain is, how inquisitive, how tolerant. I realized these really are British attitudes. And that I myself am very British in my attitudes.' Daniela then reflects on the experiences of her mum, and how these subsequently informed her own experiences about race and identity: 'Her Colombian heritage has always been about culture rather than race.'[12] Thinking solely in terms of race, without taking into account the cultural differences between and within races, results in a myopic view of identity.

Even in the western hemisphere, in nations that are geographically close to America, race varies from country to country. Whenever Henry Louis Gates, the professor of Afro-American Studies at Harvard, asks a black Cuban person how he defines himself, they would reply to Gates, 'I'm a Cuban who's black.' African-Americans, by contrast, usually say, 'I'm black and I'm an American.'[13] The Cuban defines himself primarily by his nationality; his race is secondary. In Brazil, meanwhile, there are more than 100 different categories that people use to describe what colour they are, from mestizo to mulatto, even though in America all these groups of people would simply be referred to as black. In Mexico many of the black people there simply call themselves *moreno*, which means a shade of brown, and they have a colour taxonomy in which there are sixteen shades of black.

Santo Domingo, the capital city of the Dominican Republic, was the first European city to be founded in the New World and the first to import African slaves. In the modern-day Dominican Republic, 90 per cent of people are black, or at least would be considered black in America.[14] But they typically refer to themselves as *indio*. And they see the motherland as Spain rather than Africa. Ask a Dominican and he or she will tell you, 'I'm not black, I'm Dominican.' But if they travel to New York, for instance, everyone there would consider them black. Contrast that with Haiti, the country that is cheek-by-jowl with the Dominican Republic, occupying the same island. Haiti launched the first successful slave revolt in history, and Haitians consider themselves proudly African. The native language of Dominicans is Spanish; the native language of Haitians is Kreyòl – a Creole language with a grammar shaped by West African languages.

Being bound by a fixed nation of race stops us positively acknowledging distinctive cultural expressions that transcend racial categories. As Daniela, the young woman whose mother comes from Colombia, puts it: 'People of my generation often discuss being a person of colour in Britain in the context of race and specifically in relation to Whiteness. We talk a lot about our oppression; it's how we bond. I get this, but it can sometimes feel a bit limiting.'[15] She adds that 'people of colour should bond not just around negative experiences with white people, but also around positive experiences connected to their various cultures'.

In Haiti, a country that imported more than 700,000 slaves and was considered the pearl of the Antilles by the French Empire, they still celebrate many of the customs associated with native African cultures, such as Voodoo.[16] But the black Haitian population has been crucially renewed by other cultural influences – both from Europe and from the indigenous communities of Haiti. Many black communities in north-eastern Brazil follow a syncretic religion called Candomblé, which is a fusion of native African religions and Roman Catholicism. When we think of the term 'race' we shouldn't lose sight of what makes it mean something else to different communities, such as culture or religion or nationality, and we shouldn't hold so fixed an idea of it that we lose sight of the cultural diversity that is encompassed by the term: race means different things to different people. It is the tip of a much thicker iceberg.

* * *

Afua Hirsch was brought up in a spacious house in the lush suburb of Wimbledon, in south-west London, educated at a private girls' school, spent her summer holidays in the Alps, studied at Oxford University, trained as a barrister, worked as a print journalist for the *Guardian* and as a broadcast journalist for Sky News, wrote a bestselling non-fiction book about race and identity and is now a professor of journalism in California. Yet, growing up, she felt a gaping hole in her identity.[17]

Hirsch's experiences are illustrative of broader forces at work. 'When it came to my identity,' she writes in her bestselling memoir-cum-polemic, *Brit(ish)*, 'I felt impoverished. I longed to be around other black people, to have a sense of black culture and community, to see a flicker of recognition in a person's face when I told them my name. But everyone around us was white.'[18] So she made a conscious decision to embrace black culture: at fifteen she began to collect the works of Toni Morrison, Chinua Achebe, Ama Ata Aidoo, Caryl Phillips and James Baldwin. She devoured black American films like *The Best Man* and *Love & Basketball*. This cultural diet, she was convinced, would compensate for her deprived identity.

Hirsch, like Appiah and Adekoya and my neighbour Paul, is mixed-race. Her father is of German-Jewish and Yorkshire heritage. Her mother, meanwhile, like Appiah's father, comes from a Ghanaian background. Despite Hirsch's many privileges, her childhood was not a picnic. She describes how, for instance, the younger children at school thought she was the most intimidating girl because of her racial difference. In her late teens, when she visited her best friend in a boutique shop in Wimbledon Village, she was told she couldn't come in because the manager said she was putting off the other customers. These experiences showed that race was something she couldn't avoid. 'In Britain,' she writes, 'we are taught not to see race. We are told that race does not matter. We have convinced ourselves that if we can contort ourselves into a form of blindness, then issues of identity will quietly disappear.'[19] But they won't.

When Afua was twenty-three she fell in love with a black man. Sam, a dark-skinned black man from a working-class background, who later became her husband, grew up on the other side of London in terms of geography, wealth and culture, in a deprived part of Tottenham in north London. Despite the material advantages Hirsch had over Sam, she was envious of his background: 'I was profoundly shocked by the material deprivation he experienced growing up, but when it comes to identity, I tell him, he was born with the equivalent of a silver spoon. Because when it comes to the black British experience, Sam's world is the epitome.'[20] His parents are first-generation immigrants from an African country. He comes from inner-city London. He is 'authentically' black. 'Sam's generation' of black people, Hirsch writes, 'created a subculture of almost unparalleled influence; a black, inner-city language and grime-music scene that has since the end of the century been progressively taking on the world.' Sam is confident in his black identity, whereas she was insecure. In Wimbledon she is the 'black girl'. But outside Wimbledon, in the streets of inner-city London, she is 'the rich girl who speaks "like a white person"'. And whenever she visited Ghana as a young woman, she was considered white: they called her *obruni*, which means a white person.[21] Growing up, she was unable even to correctly pronounce her first name.

Hirsch describes herself in her book as 'the eternal outsider'. She writes that she made herself appealing to the institutions that she wanted to accept her – like school, university and work. But she secretly yearned for another form of identity: black culture, black stories, 'black wisdom' and 'black role models'. An identity that would explain, and overcome, her sense of dislocation. She desperately wanted a deeper sense of blackness. This explains why, when she was a teenager, she sometimes said she was from Jamaica, 'attempting to link myself to connotations of weed, reggae, jerk chicken and urban youth culture, not an African country, associated instead with unpronounceable names, famine and psychotic dictators'. When she was a child she wanted to change her name from Afua to Caroline.[22]

Hirsch's ambiguous racial identity means that she's more (rather than less) interested in exploring questions of identity: 'It's not the muddled inheritance itself that is the problem. There is no such thing as racial purity in any event.' Furthermore:

> *The British unease at acknowledging identity is at its most visible in the tendency to celebrate the rise of interracial relationships and mixed-race people, as evidence that race and identity has somehow 'gone away'. People with mixed heritage aren't less interested in defining their identity, as some people have mistakenly assumed, but are often more so. They need to be allowed to define the way they see themselves, so that they can define themselves as British as well.*[23]

Ultimately, her 'identity started from a place of feeling "other" and alien, it evolved in conditions of prejudice and unfairness, and then grew and blossomed into something I cherish, that enriches my relationship with Britain, my country, that helps me to see nuances, truths and opportunities here that I would perhaps have been blind to otherwise'.

Hirsch thinks that 'for someone like me, Britishness contains the threat of exclusion. An exclusion only made more sinister – after so many years of searching – that there is nowhere else to go.' Britain is her home. She has Ghanaian ancestry, but Ghana is a foreign country. The people over there remind her of that. She moved to Senegal for two years after graduating from Oxford University to live and work, but she returned to Britain. Hirsch has ultimately found her sense of identity in Britain – imperfect as it is – not by looking for an idealized identity in black African culture, or more notably in black American culture, but by accepting that she is indivisibly black and British.

Blackness and Britishness are not in tension. Being mixed-race is not a muddle. We need to discard the reductive and abstract notion of race that discounts contexts like culture and nationality in favour of a subtler notion: one that reflects the realities of black people rather than twisting them beyond recognition by emphasizing the illusory notion of an authentic black identity.

Bernardine Evaristo is similar to Hirsch in some respects. She was born in London to one black African parent and one white British one. But she grew up in far humbler surroundings – Woolwich, not Wimbledon; a state school and not a private school; and a big rather than small family. And for many years she was an obscure poet and playwright. But she is now part of the literary establishment. When Evaristo won the Booker Prize in 2019 for *Girl, Woman, Other* – which she shared with Margaret Atwood's *The Testaments* – she became the first black British person, and the first black woman, to win the award. After more than twenty years of published work, and forty years of working in the arts, she has now reached the summit of the literary world: professor of creative writing at Brunel University, Booker Prize-winning novelist, literary critic for the *Guardian* and the *New Statesman*, editor for Penguin Random House of a new collection of fiction and non-fiction books by black British authors, and now president of the Royal Society of Literature. She is the first person who didn't go to Oxford, Cambridge or Eton to be president of the RSL.[24]

Like Afua Hirsch, Evaristo was embarrassed to be black as a child. 'I'd have killed to be white,' she writes in her memoir *Manifesto*, 'with long blonde hair, of course, the beauty ideal. I come from a generation of black girls who used to put cardigans on our heads so that we could flick our "long" hair over our shoulder.' She was especially embarrassed by the dark skin of her father; when she saw him on the street, she would pretend she didn't recognize him. He didn't teach the children how to speak his native language, Yoruba, because he wanted them to assimilate into British society. 'Years ago,' she writes, 'I tried to learn Yoruba at evening school, and didn't get much further than counting to ten.'[25] Growing up in a suburban area, with a father who wasn't offering her an avenue to his native Yoruba culture, and in a society that was either indifferent or hostile to her black identity, she looked to America for a positive conception of a black identity: 'There was nothing in the British society of my suburban childhood that endorsed the concept of blackness as something positive, other than the music coming out of America such as The Supremes, The Jackson 5, Stevie Wonder and The Four Tops.'[26]

Evaristo was an inquisitive girl who loved English. But she failed two of her A-levels and didn't receive any advance money for her first two books, a poetry collection entitled *Island of Abraham*, which was published in 1994 by a small press, and *Lara*, an autobiographical novel published in 1997. She was also rejected by the National Youth Theatre when she was young, but she won a place at Rose Bruford College, a drama school in Sidcup, south-east London. After she left drama school, she began to move in black social circles. There she:

encountered the notion of the Authentic
Black, to which I did not measure up. Some
folk had very clear ideas about what this
involved, and instructed me on what to
think, how to speak, how to dress, how to
dance, who to date and what to write. It
was a reductive and laughable attempt to
essentialize the concept of black-ness. All
billion plus black people in the world should
be fans of reggae – really?[27]

Evaristo adds that 'there isn't a singular black culture or community. We are not homogeneous and cannot be reduced to a few reductive tropes.'

She was nevertheless politicized by race. 'My political voice was first developed,' she writes, 'during those theatre years as we fought a long-running battle against the forces who didn't want us to exist.'[28] Although she still worries about contemporary racism, she writes that she can 'categorically state that this is not the nation of my early life, where discrimination could not be contested through a court of law and the establishment felt like an impenetrable fortress'. Her own life is testament to the fact that this fortress can be breached.

I have distant cousins who, like Paul, are mixed-race and who, like Afua Hirsch and Bernardine

Evaristo, were brought up in England as the children of one West African parent and one white British parent. But they grew up in surroundings that were different from Hirsch's Wimbledon home and closer to Evaristo's deprived setting: they were raised by a single mother in Leicester, and they went to impoverished state schools.

When my dad was twenty, he moved to England to study law. This was in seventies Britain. The exuberant optimism of the sixties had thinned out; it was the decade of inflation and the Winter of Discontent and the National Front and football hooliganism. A man my dad called Uncle Alfred was living in London. Alfred had married a white woman of Jewish ancestry who was a devout Christian. They met at a church school in London during the early sixties, as the final wave of *Windrush* immigrants was on its way, and as immigration restrictions began to be introduced. Very soon after they first met, Alfred proposed to her. They subsequently had four children together. But by the time my dad had arrived, the couple had split up. All four of these children are adults now. And all of them have always proudly identified as black, even though they only visited Nigeria, the homeland of their father, for the first time as adults. None of them speaks the native language of their father: Yoruba. Nevertheless, they still cling to a proud black identity. They are black because they grew up in a society that designated them as such, but to the people in the country where their black father came from, this fiercely held identity would dissolve: many Nigerians would consider them white. Their racial identity is not fundamentally rooted in their Africanness: many Africans don't consider them as their own, and they don't speak any native African languages. Their identity emerges in fact from their British context: they consider themselves to be black because they grew up in Britain. Trying to disentangle their Britishness from their blackness is like trying to remove a lump of sugar that has already been dissolved in a cup of tea.

What unites my cousins and me is our British context: our accents, our intuitive sense of the British landscape, our sense of humour, and our moral and cultural assumptions. But within this unity there are divisions. I can understand Yoruba, while they cannot. I was born in Nigeria and moved to Britain, whereas they have lived in Britain since birth. There is space within the black British identity for me and them.

Racial thinking is limited by the fact that racial categories don't capture the full range of humanity. But we are still attached to it because we are creatures that crave identity. The writer Kenan Malik astutely notes the dilemma in his book *Not So Black and White*: 'We also live in an age in which our thinking is saturated with racial ideology and the embrace of difference. The more we despise racial thinking, the more we cling to it. It is like an ideological version of Stockholm Syndrome.'[29] How do we resolve this? One important way is to accept that such identities need to be treated with subtlety rather than dogmatism. As Appiah writes:

> *Our largest cultural identities can free us only if we recognize that we have to make their meanings together and for ourselves. You do not get to be Western without choosing your way among myriad options, just as you do not get to be Christian or Buddhist, American or Ghanaian, gay or straight, even a man or a woman, without recognizing that each of those identities can be lived in more than one way.*[30]

The same is true of being black. There is more than one way to be black. Our 'lived experiences' are so different. As Appiah puts it: 'Talk of lived experience should be used not to end conversations but to begin them.'[31] There is no single black British voice. Despite all of this, there is something (or there are some things) distinctive about being black and British. There are some cultural affinities – a shared music, a shared language, shared cultural references, a shared sense of humour, shared national sports teams, a shared Britishness. Being black and British, in short, is not the same thing as being black and from another part of the world. But the concept of identity is frustrated by its reliance on authenticity. And so before we can consider a shared identity, we must now reflect upon the point of this book: what, exactly, is black and British?

9

BLACK AND BRITISH

What does it mean to be black and British? I got a sense of this when I first met Martha in the final week before lockdown. This was my first week working in a south-east London secondary school. My job was to teach English literature to disadvantaged kids there. I did it in either small groups or in one-to-one sessions. I taught a class of kids in person for that week, and then after lockdown was enforced throughout Britain, all teaching went online. I enjoyed my first and only personal interaction with Martha on a Tuesday: she was a confident and funny fifteen-year-old girl. But the teaching experience only made a profound impression on me during the subsequent period of lockdown, when I could only hear her voice. It reflected back to me the slice of Britain that I grew up with. It sounded like people I knew. I first taught her a few months before the murder of George Floyd and, looking back, this experience of teaching showed me what it meant to be black and British. In order to consider black British people fully, though, we need to consider the nature of the British nation.

What makes a nation? I am not going to give an authoritative definition of what constitutes a nation; there are whole books dedicated to this. For the purpose of this chapter, I will only give an impression of it. The political scientist Benedict Anderson famously called nations 'imagined communities'.[1] Is a nation simply a group of people who live together within a particular designated space? This seems like a very loose definition: if a group of people simply live together, without anything else to bond them, why should they care for each other? Or is a nation another way of describing an ethnicity? Can a particular ethnic group constitute an entire nation? Nationalism, as the American historian Jill Lepore points out, is a recent phenomenon: it is an artefact of the modern world.[2] The past was characterized by empires and city states, village communities and principalities. Not nations. This is no longer the case: we now live in a world of nations.

Lepore distinguishes between ethnic nationalism – the sort defined by one singular ethnicity – and a more inclusive form: civic nationalism. In an American context, in particular, ethnic nationalism is strange, because America has been profoundly shaped by large-scale successive waves of immigration: the British and the Dutch in the seventeenth and eighteenth centuries; the Germans, the Scandinavians and the Irish in the middle of the nineteenth century; the Italians and the Jews in the late nineteenth and early twentieth centuries; and the Latinos and Asians in the second half of the twentieth century. This is not to forget the pockets of indigenous communities throughout the country, or the group that has played an important role in this book: the black Americans who were imported to the continent as slaves.

Civic nationalism makes more sense for America than ethnic nationalism. What constitutes nationhood is not a shared ethnicity, but a shared story: a set of historical narratives and institutions and cultural artefacts that unite a group of people – the 1776 Declaration of Independence, the Constitution, the Bill of Rights, the White House, the Supreme Court, the frontier, the Civil War and many more.

Britain is not America. It has had far fewer levels of immigration throughout its history than the United States. Up until the past twenty-five years it has not experienced the scale of immigration that has been the norm for America throughout that country's history. By 1991 the share of the population that was white British was almost 95 per cent, but this does not mean Britain is a culturally homogeneous nation. In fact the very make-up of the United Kingdom of Great Britain is plural rather than singular. It is made up of three distinct nations and one province or nation or territory (Northern Ireland's status is hotly disputed). England and Wales joined together in a union in 1536. England and Scotland have shared the same monarch since 1603, but have been in political union since 1707.

And even within each of these nations there is considerable diversity. There are similarities, for instance, between communities in different nations, such as between the Lowland Scots and people from Northern England – in terms of ethnicity (Anglo-Saxon and Norse), language and religion.[3] The Highland Scots, who are more Celtic in origin and culture, have historically referred to the Lowlanders as Sassenachs (another word for Saxons), while the Lowland Scots have historically referred to the Highlanders as savages. Furthermore, the Celts within Britain do not constitute one singular group: the Gaelic spoken by Scottish Highlanders, for example, is very different from the Welsh language. In Wales itself there are cultural differences between the largely English-speaking south Wales and the Welsh-speaking north Wales. There are also distinct cultural differences within England. Brummies and Scousers and Geordies and Londoners and Yorkshire people and Bristolians are not the same – and this is reflected in the very different ways in which they speak: their accents. The Liverpool accent is especially unique. Liverpool as a city has been profoundly influenced by Ireland, and is sometimes referred to as the capital of north Wales. (Liverpool football fans booed the national anthem in the 2022 FA Cup against Chelsea; and Liverpool footballer and Scouser Trent Alexander-Arnold did not sing the anthem in an England match against Hungary in June 2022.[4]) Many of us not only have a loyalty to our nation – we also have strong regional loyalties. John Clare, the magnificent Northamptonshire poet, expressed this sentiment perfectly: 'I could not fancy England larger than the part I knew.'[5]

The heterogeneity of a British – or even English – identity has been explored by many writers and thinkers. One notable example is Daniel Defoe, the distinguished eighteenth-century novelist and journalist, who expressed the diversity of English identity in his famous poem 'The True Born Englishman':

The Scot, Pict, Britain, Roman, Dane, submit,
And with the English-Saxon all unite:

And these the mixture have so close pursu'd,
The very name and memory's subdu'd.[6]

Ultimately, according to Defoe, 'A true-born Englishman's a contradiction, / In speech an irony, in fact a fiction.' If ethnicity doesn't explain the national identity of the UK, then what does?

One candidate is war. The British historian Linda Colley argues in her book *Britons* that the people of Britain came together in the eighteenth century because they were united against the threat of Catholic France. 'Time and time again,' Colley writes, 'war with France brought Britons, whether they hailed from Wales or Scotland or England, into confrontation with an obviously hostile Other and encouraged them to collectively define themselves against it. They defined themselves as Protestants struggling for survival against the world's foremost Catholic power.'[7] It was through this succession of wars with France that Britain became Britain, and this is true of many other nations. The German states in the nineteenth century finally united to one single state under the leadership of Otto von Bismarck after a succession of wars with their continental neighbours; the same is true of Italy in the middle of the nineteenth century; and it is also true of Russia's invasion of Ukraine in 2022, which – contrary to the assumptions of Putin and other Russian nationalists – has only reinforced Ukraine's national identity. But a war between Britain and a continental neighbour is very unlikely any time soon – and thank God for that. But if we don't have war to unite us, then what can?

National sport can act as a substitute for war. As the earlier example of Liverpool and Trent Alexander-Arnold shows, some of our intense regional loyalties are mediated through the sports team we support: the unique ways Liverpool fans think of themselves reflects their complicated relationship with an English identity. This regional tribalism can also bleed into nasty sectarianism. Consider, for instance, the rivalry in Glasgow between Celtic and Rangers, and how this rivalry has been animated by the hostilities between Glaswegian Catholics and Protestants.[8] Sport can whip up strong feelings of regional bonding, but it can also do the same at a national level. This bonding is often reinforced by the specific rituals of sporting teams. For example, the Haka ritual that the New Zealand national rugby team (the All Blacks) performs before every game: it is essentially a war cry in front of their opponents.[9]

Many sports are like simulated war. And if we can't get national unification through war, we can get it through sport. Football plays a similar role in this country – at least in England. When England faced Germany in the 1990 World Cup, *The Sun* newspaper had this headline: 'Help Our Boys Clout The Krauts'. When England faced Germany in the 1996 Euro Championship, the *Mirror* ran a headline saying: 'Achtung! Surrender, for you Fritz ze Euro 96 Championship is over.' Attached to the headline was a picture of Paul Gascoigne and Stuart Pearce wearing war helmets. As the journalist Ed West puts it: 'The story of Anglo-German football rivalry mirrors the real-life relationship off the pitch, with England's great inferiority complex towards their cousins across the North Sea and an often-embarrassing obsession with past military glories.'[10] The Euro 1996 championship, held in England, led to the St George Cross being commonly waved outside for the first time in the context of sport or any other context: up until then, the Union Jack was more commonly used to express national loyalty. The sort of embarrassing chauvinism on display in the British tabloids, and the racist hooliganism that characterized English football in the past, have largely disappeared, but we still express national bonding through football. In particular, one of the striking things about England's recent football tournaments has been a revival of a song that was popular in the Euro 1996 tournament: 'Three Lions' by David

Baddiel, Frank Skinner and the Lightning Seeds. The tone of the lyrics – 'It's coming home, it's coming home, it's coming! Football's coming home' – is less an arrogant assertion of superiority than a plaintive cry for the return of a lost glory.[11] Every other year in summer now we gather in pubs or at home to cheer our nation on and sing that song.

Another striking thing about the England national team is the number of black players on it. And this is not a recent phenomenon. John Barnes, Paul Ince, Ian Wright, Ashley Cole, David James, Rio Ferdinand: all of these players and many more have served England admirably. Younger England players include Marcus Rashford and Bukayo Saka. Both are black and British. But both embody another aspect of unity that Linda Colley identified as essential to the nation: the Protestant religion. Both Rashford and Saka are Christians. They not only represent a link to Britain's future; they also represent a link to its past.

Religion, as Colley emphasized, was once an integral part of national unity: the English were different from each other, and different from the Scots and the Welsh, but we were all Protestants against a Catholic France. But in Britain today we are an increasingly irreligious society. A British Social Attitudes Survey from 2018, for example, concluded that this decline in religious affiliation is 'one of the most important trends in post-war history'.[12] But Christianity – that link to the past – is not completely dead. There is still a part of Britain where its flame lingers on. The future of the Christian religion in Britain is to be found not in the provinces of the nation, but in the most multicultural part of Europe: inner-city London. And it is being sustained not by native white British people, but by African immigrant communities.

The England and Arsenal footballer Bukayo Saka embodies the continuing legacy of Christianity in Britain, as it declines rapidly amongst the white population of the country. The twenty-one-year-old has had a redemptive story since he missed the losing penalty in the Euro 2020 final; he has been the brightest star in a rejuvenated Arsenal team and a major player in the England national team. In a video for *GQ* in April 2022, to coincide with being on the cover of the magazine, Saka listed ten things he can't live without. He included an iPad, a portable music speaker, some Twix chocolate, a football, a PlayStation, trainers and moisturizer: all the things you'd expect any sporty young man to be proud of possessing. But he also included something else – a Bible that was gifted to him by his father. 'Religion is a big part of my life,' Saka says in the video, 'obviously

I'm a strong believer in God.'[13] By 'religion', he of course means Christianity. And the use of 'obviously' is striking: why is it obvious that he would be a strong believer in God, as a young person born and bred in the capital city of a Western European nation? Well, it is obvious to him because of his family: Saka comes from a Nigerian family, and for many black African communities in Britain – as it was for many white British people in the past – Christianity is fundamental to their sense of identity.

Saka embodies a fascinating nexus: the relationship between a modern black British identity and Christianity – a religion that was introduced to anglophone West Africa by the British. The fact that Christianity is sustained by black Africans, while it is dying out throughout much of Britain, reflects something called 'the pizza effect'. The pizza was once a basic dish found in different pockets of Italy: a flat bread spread with tomato sauce; no toppings. When immigrants from Sicily and southern Italy moved to America between the late nineteenth and early twentieth century, they introduced pizza to Americans. And these Italian-Americans, on the streets of New York and Philadelphia and Chicago, gave this basic dish a renewed colour: it became a food of multiple toppings and textures. After the First World War, pizza was reintroduced back to

Italy. And it became 'pizza': not just a flat baked bread with some tomato sauce, but a national dish of magnificent variation.[14] Something similar could be said of Christianity today.

The most vigorous forms of Christianity are found in areas where immigrants live. More specifically, it is a largely West African population that fills the pews of decaying churches from Peckham to Woolwich; that renovates new churches in Brixton and Lewisham; and that volunteers for Christian centres and charities across the capital. If you want a solid sense of the sacred, a connection to Britain's ancient Christian past, then you are more likely to find it while eating jollof rice in a big tent in Kennington than eating Yorkshire pudding in a small room in Harrogate.

People pray more in London than anywhere else in the country.[15] In the city 56 per cent of Christians pray regularly; only 32 per cent outside it do so. London is more Christian today than it was during Margaret Thatcher's time as prime minister. According to David Goodhew, the director of ministerial practice at Cranmer Hall in Durham University, between 1979 and 2012 there was a 50 per cent rise in the number of churches in the capital city. Many of them were built in boroughs of London with a large black population, such as Southwark. The political scientist Eric Kaufmann points out that secularization is 'almost entirely a white British phenomenon'.[16] When the share of white British people decreases in an area, secularization also slows down. The number of white British people who ticked 'no religion' in the census rose from 15.4 per cent in 2001 to 28 per cent in 2011. And 59.3 per cent of the population in the 2011 census identified as Christian; this dropped to 46.2 per cent in the 2021 census. With the 2021 census, the majority of the British population now lacks any religious affiliation.[17] By contrast, the number of black Africans who ticked 'no religion' between 2001 and 2011 rose by only a tiny amount: from 2.3 per cent to 2.9 per cent. It is black Africans who are sustaining Christianity in London. In Southwark alone, there are more than 250 black-majority churches. If conservatives want to renew Christianity in Britain, then the most effective way is not to rely on public pronouncements by Justin Welby and Pope Francis. It would be by introducing an open-borders immigration policy for all the African countries that Britain once colonized.

Ask many black Africans in Britain today, and they would emphasize the importance of Christianity to their identity. In general, black British people are more than twice as likely to say religion is very important to them. Most black British believers are Christian. As Jimi Famurewa puts it, 'For me and so many others, our Black African identity is inextricably linked to faith.'[18] Yet the centrality of Christianity to black British identity is not spoken about enough. Saka treasures his music and his football. But on his Instagram account his name is not Bukayo Saka, but 'God's Child' (at least at the time of writing). Christianity can accommodate tension. Its central figure is both a man who was abused and spat on and crucified, like a slave, but also a figure of transcendent divinity. What can be more beautifully Christian than the fact that its future, in the bosom of what was once the largest empire in the world, is being sustained by communities that were once colonized?

Another thing that unites black people of various backgrounds, and connects black people with other races and ethnic groups in Britain, is music. Jeffrey Boakye, for instance, has been able to find, through popular music, a way of uniting black Africans and black Caribbean people. One example of this is grime music: 'Grime has been the soundtrack to this unification, inviting black Londoners (at first) to unite under an umbrella of Jamaican cultural cool.'[19] The godfathers of grime music were largely black Caribbean men from East London, such as Dizzee Rascal, Wiley and Kano. But many of the biggest stars of the genre today are men of black African origin, such as Stormzy, Little Simz and Dave.

And it's now no longer a musical genre confined to inner-city black kids in London; grime is listened to by young people from across the country, and of all races. At the 2019 Glastonbury music festival, Dave – a twenty-one-year-old black British musician of Nigerian descent, who was born and bred in south London – invited a fifteen-year-old white boy in a bucket hat from Wells, Somerset, called Alex Mann, to rap with him a song entitled 'Thiago Silva'.[20] Alex did a very good job.

The language used in grime is also an increasingly popular dialect of English, and this is another instance of the intertwining of a black British identity with a larger British identity: the very way we speak. According to Matt Gardner, a professor of linguistics at Oxford, Multicultural London English (MLE) will be the dominant dialect spoken in this country by the end of this century – words like 'peng' and 'bare', which derived from immigrant communities in pockets of inner London, will soon be part of the normal vocabulary up and down England's green and pleasant land.[21] There was a time when it was simply Jamaican patois, but Multicultural London English is now a mixture of Jamaican, cockney and African intonations. More than that, it incorporates elements of Greek and Turkish. It is truly cosmopolitan. And it's not spoken just by black or Asian kids. As the example of Alex from Somerset shows, many white kids from rural England can speak it, too. Rebecca Mead, an English *New Yorker* staff writer, has described how her American-born teenage son started using this dialect very soon after she and her family moved to London from New York.[22]

Multicultural London English isn't only used in music, but also in television, and one of the best TV shows of recent years, Michaela Coel's *I May Destroy You*, brilliantly captures the cultural intermixing that underpins this dialect. It also offers one of the most insightful accounts of contemporary black British life. In the show, both white and black characters speak MLE as their mother tongue. The actors pinpoint certain Caribbean and West African intonations: they use *Rah* to express shock or indignation, while Kwame, a British-Ghanaian character, says *oya* – a Nigerian (Yoruba) word meaning 'hurry up' – to the other characters when they're preparing for a party.[23] The drama abounds with traumatic and violent scenes, but there's also humour, in particular that combination of self-deprecating wit and awkwardness so characteristic of British comedy. As the writer Bolu Babalola puts it, in her review of the show: 'Sophisticatedly woven themes of consent, sexual politics, and social media's power to amplify, soothe, and subsume are not presented within a neutral vacuum, but rather within a specifically Black British sphere.'[24] This rich mixing of styles and registers is typical of MLE itself. It's more than simply a dialect; it illustrates black Britain's increasing influence on mainstream British identity and its openness to other immigrant influences. In one especially striking scene in *I May Destroy You*, Arabella, the protagonist, is in a doctor's surgery. The doctor calls her 'Afro-Caribbean', and she's immediately offended by this. She responds, 'No, I'm not Afro-Caribbean, I am British-African.' She adds that there is both 'unity and a distinction' when it comes to describing black British people.[25] The existence of a dialect like MLE shouldn't be taken to imply that black British people have lost track of their specific cultural origins. Rather, it means they've proudly combined their culture with other black cultures within a wider British context.

In his famous essay 'The Lion and the Unicorn', George Orwell asked: 'What can the England of 1940 have in common with the England of 1840? But then, what have you in common with the child of five whose photograph your mother keeps on the mantelpiece? Nothing, except that you happen to be the same person.'[26] The black British population is a continuation of Britain. The skin pigmentation may look different, the accents may have altered, but the inheritance is the same. My intuitive sensibility is a British one. I have been shadowed by the landscape of London; I speak English with a south-London register. When I travel, on a train or in a car, through the rural landscape that courses through England, I respond with a mixture of awe and familiarity. Awe at the great beauty of it. Familiarity because I have – or feel that I have – seen it before.

As Jill Lepore demonstrated, civic nationalism is not about ethnicity. It is about a larger national story. Black people are a part of the British story. Through sport, religion, music, television and language, black communities are linked to a British identity. They are renewing Britain's culture and institutions. Black people in the UK represent a continuation of, rather than a break from, Britishness.

But some people, like Kehinde Andrews, think a black identity and Britishness are in tension. In a 2021 interview with the *Guardian*, Andrews expressed the most perfect articulation of what a friend of mine has coined 'woke Powellism': 'the biggest mistake we make in Britain,' Andrews said of black people in Britain, 'is that we really do try to integrate into society.'[27] Like Enoch Powell, Andrews is opposed to integration. The nation is so irredeemably racist, he thinks, that any attempt to incorporate black people into the mainstream endangers their lives. The only way for black people to thrive in Britain is through alternative spaces. Andrews was one of the people listed by Vernon and Osborne in their book *100 Great Black Britons*.

But Andrews is wrong. Most black and ethnic-minority people are integrating into British society and are optimistic about the future of race relations. In the wake of George Floyd's murder, the researcher Renie Anjeh conducted a poll for YouGov in November 2020, which found that, as he put it in *The Times*, there is 'diversity of opinion on various issues, some of which do not fit neatly with popular preconceptions held by many'.[28] More than half of ethnic-minority voters think race relations have improved over the past fifty years. And they have good reason for thinking so. In 1983 more than 50 per cent of British people would not marry someone from a different race. By 2020 more than 90 per cent would accept their child marrying someone from a different race. Nearly 80 per cent of the respondents believed it was important for immigrants to integrate into society, and this figure was highest for black people and those born outside the UK: black British people value the importance of integration. And so does the rest of the British population.

According to a different Ipsos Mori poll in June 2020, 89 per cent of British people claim they would be happy for a child to marry someone from a different ethnic group (and 70 per cent strongly agree).[29] In January 2009 it was 75 per cent (with only 41 per cent strongly agreeing). And 93 per cent disagree with the statement 'to be truly British you have to be white' (with 84 per cent strongly disagreeing). In October 2006, 82 per cent disagreed (55 per cent strongly). Ten per cent agreed with the statement; 3 per cent do now.

Others accept that black people have integrated into British society, but they view this as a tragedy. In 2011, for instance, the Tudor historian David Starkey appeared on BBC's *Newsnight* to discuss the London riots with Owen Jones and Dreda Say Mitchell. On that programme Starkey claimed that the 'whites are turning into blacks'.[30] He was referring in particular to Multicultural London English. There was uproar about his comment, but he was not entirely wrong. The problem is that Starkey saw this as a form of decadence. I see it as a positive thing: the fact of cultural intermixing. Black identity is not alien to Britishness. It is encompassed by it.

* * *

What will a more effective form of anti-racist politics look like? It will have to be two things: collaborative and specific. When it comes to the relationship between the police and black British people, for instance, the police will have to do their part in curbing racism within their ranks: investigations into police misconduct will have to be done in a way that is utterly transparent to the victimized party. Many young black people don't trust the police, and you can understand why: the legacy of institutional police racism still has traces today, in terms of hostile responses to some black people who have been unfairly suspected of a crime. A small minority of activists and academics believe the police should be abolished; it is ineradicably corrupted, they argue, by racism. An argument like this is thoroughly misguided: the people who will suffer most from the eradication of the police are the young black men sucked into crime and vulnerable to the brutal violence of criminal subcultures. The police and particular black communities need to build a better relationship together, precisely *because* black lives matter.

The police could go into schools and local youth centres in an open and generous manner. Likewise, black activists should set up events and talks where young black people in impoverished communities can be invited to interact with senior members of the police. This should be done in order that these groups can develop a greater degree of trust and can bond with each other. The police also need to do a better job of recruiting from the areas they serve: this localist approach will demonstrate that they are not an alien force imposing control from somewhere distant, but are tightly embedded within their communities.

In terms of education, rather than generalizing about how black people do in terms of exam results and discipline, we need to be more specific in our focus. Many activists argue that teachers and staff in school are unfairly hostile to black students. But the true picture is more complex than this. It is black Caribbean students who are excluded at a high rate, not black African students. We need to ponder why this is the case. Even controlling for class, the disparity between black Caribbean and black African students still exists. One reason is perhaps differing family formation: black African boys are more likely to have more role models in their lives. Young men, in particular, need male role models. Activists should thus encourage more long-lasting mentoring schemes. This can even be done in-house: so schools should encourage high-achieving and well-disciplined older black students to mentor the younger black students who pose red flags, in terms of behaviour and discipline.

These suggestions do not ignore the individual instances of teachers behaving in a racist manner to black students: that still happens and should be punished accordingly. Schools are not always safe for black kids. The example of Child Q is instructive. She is the vulnerable teenage girl in Hackney who was strip-searched by the police and treated with gross negligence by her school.[31] Nevertheless, the vast majority of teachers are well-meaning, and a deeper engagement with the issues at hand on the part of the teachers is important. Only a sharper focus on the cultural differences within the black British population can genuinely enable activists to improve the chances of the black kids who are struggling at school.

In terms of more black people getting into the arts sector and publishing, a bigger question ought to be: How can we make these professions economically viable for talented young people from non-affluent backgrounds? This is a class issue as much as it is a race issue. It shouldn't just be a case of how we can get more black people into arts and publishing; it should also be about how we can get working-class young people of all backgrounds into these professions. However, if these professions continue to pay their younger staff badly, continue to be disproportionately located in extremely expensive cities like London, and continue to cultivate a culture of nepotism that will be alienating to newcomers, then a more fundamental question needs to be asked: Why should under-represented talented and creative young people be encouraged to get into these professions in the first place?

Deeper introspection needs to take place within the creative industries and publishing than simply stating, 'We need more racial diversity.' What they need is to create a more attractive economic environment for newcomers. This, of course, isn't entirely their fault: it speaks to a wider issue about the things our economy and our society values. Young black people who are passionate about getting into these industries should definitely be encouraged to join them. I am all for events at schools and universities led by publishing and arts companies that specifically target marginalized groups; but the young people should also be clear-sighted about the potential financial risks involved. If the claim that black lives matter is meaningful, it needs to be honest about the consequences of particular schemes for greater diversity; simply promoting greater racial diversity is not good enough, without caring whether such schemes will genuinely improve the material conditions of black people.

We don't live in a post-racial society. But we have made advances. We should use this to inspire further progress. This means, among other things, honest and grounded discussions that are rooted in the particular experiences of black British communities. George Floyd's killing opened up a new and important cultural space. Many older black Britons felt able to speak openly about the painful racism they faced in the past (and which some still continue to face today). It's extremely important that they – and others – continue to have the confidence to speak about these experiences, not only because it enables them to receive justice but also because the wider the knowledge of genuine instances of racism, the less likely we are to be complacent about racial progress. The response to Floyd's death has also revealed the significant growth in expectations among many younger black people on matters of race and equality. Most are far more sensitive to racial prejudice than their parents or grandparents felt able to be, and are much less inclined to keep their heads down or turn the other cheek. This, ironically, is a consequence of their greater integration into British society. The more British we feel, the more invested we are in this country, and the more painful it is to suffer discrimination.

Nevertheless, Britain has made great progress on matters of race, and those who imply that we haven't risk trivializing the brutal prejudice that many black Britons experienced in the past. The challenge now for some campaigners is to find ways to recognize this progress without degenerating into complacency. Acknowledging positive change, and being cautiously optimistic, are more consistent with the realities of contemporary black British life than the fatalism of some Black Lives Matter supporters. We should also accept that a person's race is not the most important thing about them. It is their humanity.

* * *

America is its own country. It has its own successes and its own problems. Some of these successes and problems are shared with other countries, but in America they are filtered through the distinctive history, institutions and cultures that constitute the American nation. I accept why we continue to think within American cultural frames: we consume so much American culture; we speak the same language. But even when two nations speak the same language, things can be lost in translation. One of these things is race.

Black British people are just that – black *and* British. The damage done by looking at race in Britain through an American perspective obscures the particular challenges some black people in Britain face, and stops us from celebrating the particular achievements some black people have made. It is also damaging to see race through an abstract or neutral perspective. We must specifically emphasize a British context.

A healthy civic society is one in which everyone – irrespective of race, religion, ethnic background or political ideology – can speak to one another with a shared sense of identity. If we lose this capacity, there is a risk that we will fracture along racial lines. This damage will be most pressing on black people. It will render them invisible. But it will negatively impact wider society, too. We will be unable to build a genuinely effective form of anti-racist politics because we will lose sight of the ability to connect with each other at a human level.

Thankfully, some of these conversations are already present in the UK today. There is a late-night programme on Channel 4 called *Unapologetic*, which is presented by two young black British women, Yinka Bokinni and Zeze Millz, and in which issues related to identity are discussed in a refreshingly open way.[32] There is a diverse range of views being aired on the show. One of the guests, for instance, is a young woman named Inaya Folarin Iman. People might be tempted to pigeonhole her as a reactionary thinker because she has previously worked as a broadcaster for the right-wing channel GB News. But she is a subtle and interesting thinker. In 2020 she founded an ideas and debate forum called the Equiano Project. It was a pleasure to spend two nights in January 2023 at a conference organized by them in Cambridge. It was called 'Towards the Common Good: Rethinking Race in the 21st Century', and it brought some of the world's leading thinkers on identity in one place: John McWhorter, Glenn Loury, Coleman Hughes, Sir Trevor Phillips, Kenan Malik, Ayishat Akanbi, Sonia Sodha and many more.[33] These writers and academics do not share the same political outlook – some are conservative, some are liberal, some are progressive. What they share, and what my book advocates, is an abiding faith in the irreducible dignity of every person, irrespective of their racial background. What they reject, and what my book also rejects, is the assumption that some racial groups like black people should be treated like children.

White people should also be able to take part confidently in these conversations. This is because racism can only be effectively addressed by all of society, not just black people. This is why open conversations about race are not well served by white guilt. If every white person sceptical about any of the claims of contemporary race orthodoxy is denounced as a racist, the conversation will always grind to a halt; we will only be left with sermonizing and finger-pointing. More to the point: the kind of stigmatizing of white people that is increasingly fashionable in some activist circles is wrong in itself. It demeans our capacity to recognize each other as individuals endowed with inherent moral worth. I am opposed to it not because I am indifferent to racial inequality. I am opposed to it because I am against racial inequality. What underpins my opposition is seeing people first as individuals, not as representatives of their race. This is not to argue that I don't see race, or that race doesn't matter. It is to argue that to define someone exclusively by their race is to acquiesce to the vision of racists. I will not stand by that.

* * *

We are an increasingly integrated society, not just through intermarriage, but also through cultural intermingling. This is particularly the case for younger people. Ordinary Britons of every kind need to find the courage to have conversations with each other that reflect this integration and are characterized by a generosity of spirit rather than by anxiety. Black and white, we need to be able to talk and listen to each other in good faith. We share a common tongue.

I am sometimes told that I speak with a south-London twang. This delights me. But if you listen carefully to it, you will notice it has been filtered by my Nigerian background: there is still a trace of West African in my accent. When I was teaching Martha in that secondary school in south-east London, I recognized that voice in her. She is a white British girl, and I was tutoring her in English literature. So we shared two inheritances. One inheritance is the glories of English literature. The other is the glories of a multi-ethnic society. As I listened to her read from Shakespeare and worked on some Dickens passages with her, I could hear beneath her south-London voice some unmistakably African intonations. To be black and British is to see yourself reflected back in wider society, to see your identity as consistent with the mainstream. Martha was white and had a bit of black in her voice; but she was still, like me, irreducibly British.

NOTES

Introduction

1. Georgia Wright, 'Here are the retailers going beyond solidarity for Black Lives Matter', *Retail Gazette*.
2. Much of the information about the reaction to the murder of George Floyd can be gleaned from this Wikipedia page: 'Reactions to the George Floyd protests'.
3. Fraser Nelson, 'The Tories are in danger of learning the wrong lessons from Boris's fall', *Telegraph*, July 2022.
4. Will Lloyd, 'Meet Britain's radical New Right', *UnHerd*, November 2022.
5. Stephen Castle, 'As Boris Johnson Stumbles, Labour Struggles to Offer a Clear Message', *The New York Times*, May 2022.
6. Helen Lewis, 'The World is Trapped in America's Culture War', *The Atlantic*, October 2020.
7. I saw this on TV, but it was also reported by Andy Hall in 'England players again take the knee... for three seconds, in World Cup match against USMNT', for *Diario AS*, November 2022.
8. Richard F. Kuisel, 'Coca-Cola and the Cold War: The French Face Americanization,

1948–1953', *French Historical Studies*, Vol. 17, No. 1 (Spring 1991), p.96.
9. The Adichie quote is from a profile by Zoe Williams, '"I believe literature is in peril": Chimamanda Ngozi Adichie comes out fighting for freedom of speech', in the *Guardian*, November 2022.
10. Aris Roussinos, 'Elon Musk must destroy Twitter', *UnHerd*, 4 November 2022.
11. Thomas Paine, *Rights of Man, Common Sense, and Other Political Writings*, Oxford World's Classics, 2008, p.19.
12. John Gray, *Black Mass: Apocalyptic Religion and the Death of Utopia*, Granta, 2008, p.160.
13. I found this in a YouTube lecture on Ukraine, 'Ukraine: From Propaganda to Reality', Chicago Humanities Festival, in 2015.
14. Henry Luce, 'The American Century', *Diplomatic History*, Vol. 23, No. 2 (Spring 1999), Oxford University Press, p.159.
15. Andrew Bacevich, *The Limits of Power: The End of American Exceptionalism*, Henry Holt & Co., 2009, p.55.
16. Janan Ganesh, 'The autocratic world will split before the

west does', *Financial Times*, 23 August 2022.

17. Alastair Bonnett, *Multiracism: Rethinking Racism in Global Context*, Polity, 2021.

18. Data taken from United Kingdom Population, Worldometer; United States Census Bureau, '2020 U.S. Population More Racially and Ethnically Diverse Than Measured in 2010'; Gov.UK website, Population of England and Wales.

19. Hugo Rifkind, 'Gangs of London series two review – I've never seen people get shot in the face in such expensive suits', *The Times*, 21 October 2022.

20. List of countries by intentional homicide rate, and abortion law in the United States by state, both from Wikipedia.

21. George Santayana, 'Materialism and Idealism in American Life', in *American Conservatism*, ed. Andrew Bacevich, Library of America, 2020, p.40.

22. Robert Hughes, 'The Decline of the City of Mahagonnay', *Nothing If Not Critical*, The Harvill Press/Panther, 1990, p.80.

23. David Rozado, 'The Increasing Prominence of Prejudice and

Social Justice Rhetoric in UK News Media', *Rozado's Visual Analytics*, 2 August 2022.

24. From the Census Results 2021.

25. David Lammy quote from Nazia Parveen and Aamna Mohdin, 'Starmer promises race equality act, a year on from George Floyd's murder', *Guardian*, 25 May 2021.

26. Information about George Floyd's life from Robert Samuels and Toluse Olorunnipa, *His Name Is George Floyd: One man's life and the struggle for racial justice*, Bantam Press, 2022, p.55.

27. Terry Allen, 'Blacks in Britain', Spring 2002 University of Rochester Frederick Douglass Project.

28. Sunder Katwala, 'The Enoch myth', *Guardian*, April 2008.

29. George Orwell, 'As I Please', *Tribune*, 3 December 1943.

30. Christopher Hitchens, *Hitch-22*, Atlantic Books, 2010, p.145.

31. 'List of US cities with large Black populations', Wikipedia.

32. Walt Whitman, 'Song of Myself', 51, on poets.org.

33. Randall Kennedy, 'Sellout: First Chapter', *The New York Times*, February 2008.

1 Double Consciousness

1. W. E. B. Du Bois, *The Souls of Black Folk*, ed. Brent Hayes Edwards, Oxford World's Classics, 2008, p.30.

2. David Levering Lewis, *W. E. B. Du Bois*, Henry Holt and Co., 2009, p.17.

3. Du Bois, *The Souls of Black Folk*, p.32.

4. Caryl Phillips, *Colour Me English*, Harvill Secker, 2011, p.7.
5. Phillips, p.10.
6. Phillips, p.21.
7. Phillips, p.25.
8. Peniel E. Joseph, *Stokely: A Life*, Civitas Books, 2014, p.26.
9. *Stokely Speaks: From Black Power to Pan-Africanism*, ed. Bob Brown, A Cappella Books, 2007, p.28.
10. Hakim Adi, *Pan-Africanism: A History*, Bloomsbury, 2018, p.112.
11. Adi, p.114.
12. Information about Nkrumah gained from Martin Meredith, *The State of Africa: A History of the Continent Since Independence*, Simon & Schuster UK, 2011, p.80.
13. Senghor information also from Meredith, p.135.
14. Adi, *Pan-Africanism*, p.135.
15. John Winthrop, 'Dreams of a City on a Hill' (1630), from The American Yawp Reader website.

2 American Integrationism

1. First Ellison quote from Robert Penn Warren, *Who Speaks for the Negro?*, Yale University Press, 2014, p.89.
2. The Cornel West and Farah Jasmine Griffin quotes are from the documentary 'Ralph Ellison: An American Journey', 2002, YouTube.
3. Biographical information about Ellison from Arnold Rampersad, *Ralph Ellison: A Biography*, Alfred A. Knopf Inc., 2007.
4. Ralph Ellison, *Invisible Man*, Penguin Modern Classics, 2001, p.5.
5. Ellison, p.60.
6. Ralph Ellison, 'What America Would Be Like Without Blacks', *Time Magazine*, 1970.
7. 'Conversation with a Native Son: Maya Angelou and James Baldwin', YouTube.
8. James Campbell, *Talking at the Gates: A Life of James Baldwin*, Faber, 1991, p.160.
9. Michael Kazin, 'A Patriotic Left', *Dissent* magazine, 2002.
10. Kazin.
11. Stanley Crouch on *The Charlie Rose Show*, November 1993 and February 1998.
12. *The Sopranos*, 'Commendatori', Season 2, Episode 4.
13. Richard Wright, *12 Million Black Voices*, Basic Books, 2002, p.30.
14. Biographical information on Albert Murray from Henry Louis Gates, 'King of Cats', *The New Yorker*, April 1996.
15. Albert Murray, *The Omni-Americans: Some Alternatives to the Folklore of White Supremacy*, Library of America, 2020, p.17.
16. Robert S. Boynton, 'The New Intellectuals', *The Atlantic*, March 1995.
17. Saul Bellow, *The Adventures of Augie March*, Penguin Modern Classics, 2001, p.3.

18. Ellison quote from Boynton, 'The New Intellectuals'.
19. Malcolm X, 'The Ballot or the Bullet' speech, April 1964.
20. Ralph Ellison, 'The World and the Jug', *Shadow and Act*, Vintage Books, 1972, p.75.
21. Ruth Koizim quote from Phoebe Kimmelman and Matthew Lloyd-Thomas, 'French in Action creator Pierre Capretz dies', *Yale Daily News*, 4 April 2014.
22. 'French in Action, Leçon 1 HD, Introduction', YouTube.
23. R. G. Collingwood, *The Principles of Art*, Oxford University Press, 1968, p.79.
24. David Macey, *Frantz Fanon: A Biography*, Verso Books, 2012.
25. Frantz Fanon, *The Wretched of the Earth*, Penguin Modern Classics, 2001, p.287.
26. Adam Shatz, 'Where Life Is Seized', *London Review of Books*, 2017.
27. Frantz Fanon, *Black Skin, White Masks*, Penguin Modern Classics, 2021, p.89.

3 Critical Race Theory

1. Malcolm X, 'If You Stick A Knife In My Back', YouTube.
2. Elaine Brown and Stokely Carmichael quotes from 'Black Power: A Discussion on the Condition of the Black Community', YouTube.
3. Ta-Nehisi Coates, *Between the World and Me*, Text Publishing Company, 2015, p.78.
4. Coates, p.89.
5. Jelani Cobb, 'The Man Behind Critical Race Theory', *The New Yorker*, September 2021.
6. Richard Delgado and Jean Stefancic, *Critical Race Theory: An Introduction*, NYU Press, 2017, p.16.
7. Derrick Bell, '*Brown v. Board of Education* and the Interest-Convergence Dilemma', *Harvard Law Review*, Vol. 93, No. 3 (January 1980).
8. Bell, *Harvard Law Review*.
9. Derrick Bell, *Faces at the Bottom of the Well: The Permanence of Racism*, Basic Books, 1993, p.56.
10. Bell, *Faces at the Bottom of the Well*, p.25.
11. Jennifer Ratner-Rosenhagen, *The Ideas That Made America: A Brief History*, Oxford University Press USA, 2019, p.34.
12. Jill Lepore, *These Truths: A History of the United States*, W. W. Norton & Co., 2018, p.508.
13. Bell, *Faces at the Bottom of the Well*, p.26.
14. Derrick Bell, *Ethical Ambition*, Bloomsbury, 2003, p.78.
15. James Baldwin, *Collected Essays*, Library of America, 1998, p.78.
16. Coates, *Between the World and Me*, p.230.
17. Christopher Rufo, 'How a Conservative Activist Invented the Conflict Over Critical Race Theory', *The New Yorker*, June 2021.
18. James Lindsay, *Race Marxism: The Truth About Critical Race Theory and Praxis*,

independently published, 2022.

19. Ernest Renan, 'What is a Nation?', text of a conference delivered at the Sorbonne on 11 March 1882, in Ernest Renan, *Qu'est-ce qu'une nation?*, Presses-Pocket, Paris, 1992 (translated by Ethan Rundell).

20. Kimberlé Crenshaw, 'Demarginalizing the Intersection of Race and Sex: A Black Feminist Critique of Antidiscrimination Doctrine, Feminist Theory and Antiracist Politics', *University of Chicago Legal Forum*, Vol. 1989, Issue 1, Article 8, 1989.

21. Jane Coaston, 'The intersectionality wars', *Vox*, 2019.

22. Kimberlé Crenshaw, 'Race to the Bottom', *The Baffler*, 2017.

23. 'Who We Are: Beyond Black and White', Institute of Art and Ideas, 2018.

24. Coleman Hughes, 'Reflections on Intersectionality', *Quillette*, 2020.

25. Thomas Sowell, *Discrimination and Disparities*, Basic Books, 2022, p.159.

26. Bayard Rustin, *Time on Two Crosses: The Collected Writings of Bayard Rustin*, Cleis Press, 2020, p.70.

27. *Students for Fair Admissions v. President and Fellows of Harvard College*, Wikipedia, 2022.

28. Robin DiAngelo, *White Fragility: Why It's So Hard for White People to Talk About Racism*, Penguin, 2019, p.23.

29. Robin DiAngelo, *Nice Racism: How Progressive White People Perpetuate Racial Harm*, Penguin, 2019, p.15.

30. DiAngelo, *Nice Racism*, p.38.

31. DiAngelo, p.188.

32. Louis Menand, 'What Our Biggest Best-Sellers Tell Us About a Nation's Soul: Reading America through more than two centuries of its favorite books', *The New Yorker*, 2021.

33. Layla F. Saad, *Me and White Supremacy: How to Recognise Your Privilege, Combat Racism and Change the World*, Quercus, 2020, p.145.

34. Ibram X. Kendi, *How to Be an Antiracist: The book that transformed the world's understanding of racism*, Bodley Head, 2019, p.202.

35. Kendi, p.123.

36. Kendi, p.162.

37. Kendi, p.165.

4 Immigration

1. Ngozi Fulani biography on Future Hackney website.

2. *BBC News*, 'Lady Susan Hussey quits over remarks to charity boss Ngozi Fulani'.

3. *BBC News*, 'Murder of Stephen Lawrence'.

4. Amelia Gentleman, '"I can't eat or sleep": The woman threatened with deportation after 50 years in Britain' re Paulette Wilson, *Guardian*, 28 November 2017.

5. Amelia Gentleman, 'They don't tell you why: Threatened with

removal after 52 years in the UK', *Guardian*, 1 December 2017.

6. Amelia Gentleman, 'Shameful: widespread outrage over man denied NHS cancer care', *Guardian*, 12 March 2018.

7. Paul Walker and Amelia Gentleman, 'Theresa May apologises for treatment of Windrush citizens', *Guardian*, April 2018.

8. Nick Hopkins and Heather Stewart, 'Amber Rudd was sent targets for migrant removal, leak reveals', *Guardian*, April 2018.

9. David Olusoga, *Black and British: A Forgotten History*, Pan Macmillan, 2017, p.412.

10. Olusoga, p.435.

11. 'Windrush – Documentary (1998): 4. A British Story', YouTube.

12. Trevor Phillips and Mike Phillips, *Windrush: The Irresistible Rise of Multi-Racial Britain*, HarperCollins, 1999, p.86.

13. George Lamming, *The Pleasures of Exile*, Pluto Press, 2005, p.78.

14. Phillips and Phillips, *Windrush*, p.67.

15. Phillips and Phillips, p.62.

16. Colin Grant, *Homecoming: Voices of the Windrush Generation*, Vintage, 2020.

17. Phillips and Phillips, *Windrush*, p.71.

18. Phillips and Phillips, p.111.

19. Phillips and Phillips, p.15.

20. Phillips and Phillips, p.17.

21. Phillips and Phillips, p.34.

22. Phillips and Phillips, p.36.

23. Clair Wills, *Lovers and Strangers: An Immigrant History of Post-War Britain*, Penguin, 2018, p.50.

24. Olusoga, *Black and British*, p.356.

25. David Olusoga, 'The Unwanted: The Secret Windrush Files', *BBC News*, iPlayer.

26. Auberon Waugh quoted in Robert Winder, *Bloody Foreigners: The Story of Immigration to Britain*, Abacus, 2013, p.147.

27. Olusoga, *Black and British*, p.360.

28. Thatcher quoted in 'Windrush – Documentary (1998): 4. A British Story', YouTube.

29. Phillips and Phillips, *Windrush*, p.45.

30. 'Windrush – Documentary (1998): 4. A British Story', YouTube.

31. Amelia Gentleman, '"I can't eat or sleep": The woman threatened with deportation after 50 years in Britain' re Paulette Wilson, *Guardian*, 28 November 2017.

5 Empire

1. BBC Poll of Greatest Britons of all time.

2. 'The Racial Consequences of Mr Churchill', Churchill College Cambridge: Churchill, Empire and Race series, 12 February 2021.

3. Virou Srilangarajah, 'We Are Here Because You Were With Us: Remembering A.

Sivanandan (1923–2018)',
Verso website, February 2018.

4. *BBC News*, 'Winston Churchill
statue: Man fined for spraying
"racist"', October 2020.

5. 'Racial views of Winston
Churchill', Wikipedia.

6. Caroline Elkins, *Legacy of
Violence: A History of the British
Empire*, Bodley Head, 2022,
p.10.

7. Elkins, p.14.

8. Elkins, p.18.

9. Elkins, p.24.

10. Peter Mitchell, *Imperial
Nostalgia: How the British
Conquered Themselves*,
Manchester University Press,
2021; and Kojo Karam,
*Uncommon Wealth: Britain and
the Aftermath of Empire*, John
Murray, 2022.

11. Eric Williams quote from
Fara Dabhoiwala, 'Imperial
Delusion', *The New York
Review of Books*, July 2021.

12. Quotes of Enlightenment
thinkers from Kehinde
Andrews, *The New Age of
Empire: How Racism and
Colonialism Still Rule the World*,
Penguin, 2021.

13. Karl Marx, 'The Future Results
of British Rule in India', *New
York Daily Tribune*, 8 August
1853.

14. John Gray, *Black Mass:
Apocalyptic Religion and the
Death of Utopia*, Penguin,
2008.

15. Walter Benjamin, 'On the
Concept of History'.

16. Jonathan Israel, *Radical
Enlightenment: Philosophy
and the Making of Modernity
1650–1750*, Oxford University
Press, 2002.

17. John Darwin, 'Lowering
the flag: How the British
justified imperial violence to
themselves', *Times Literary
Supplement*, 15 April 2022.

18. Chinua Achebe, *Things Fall
Apart*, Penguin Classics, 2006.

19. Meredith, *The State of Africa*,
p.74.

20. Sunil Khilnani, 'The British
Empire Was Much Worse Than
You Realize', *The New Yorker*,
28 March 2022.

21. Andrews, *The New Age of
Empire*, p.124.

22. Andrews, p.128.

23. C. L. R. James, *The Black
Jacobins: Toussaint L'Ouverture
and the San Domingo
Revolution*, Penguin, 2001.

24. Sathnam Sanghera,
*Empireland: How Imperialism
Has Shaped Modern Britain*,
Viking, 2021.

25. Stephen Bush, 'Why the
British empire alone cannot
explain the politics of the
present', *New Statesman*, 10
February 2021.

26. British Social Attitudes Survey,
'Brexit and immigration: A
country divided', 2017.

27. Simon Heffer, *Like The Roman:
The Life of Enoch Powell*,
Weidenfeld & Nicolson, 1998.

28. European Agency for
Fundamental Rights, 'Being
Black in the EU – Second
European Union Minorities
and Discrimination Survey',
2017.

29. Keiron Pim, *Endless Flight:
The Life of Joseph Roth*, Granta
Books, 2022.

30. David Olusoga, 'The toppling
of Edward Colston's statue is
not an attack on history. It

is history', *Guardian*, 8 June 2020.

31. Olusoga, *Guardian*.
32. Tom Lamont, 'How the trial of the Colston Four was won: The inside story', *New Statesman*, 2 April 2022.
33. YouGov, 'Do you approve or disapprove of protesters in Bristol pulling down the statue of Edward Colston?', 8 June 2020.
34. Michael Savage, 'Four in five people in the UK believe in being "woke" to race and social justice', *Guardian*, May 2022.
35. 'Attitudes to race and inequality in Great Britain', Ipsos Mori, June 2020.
36. Patrick Vernon and Angelina Osborne, *100 Great Black Britons*, Robinson, 2021, p.11.
37. Olusoga in *100 Great Black Britons*, p.5.
38. Vernon and Osborne, *100 Great Black Britons*, p.34.
39. Tony Diver, 'Winston Churchill viewed positively by just a fifth of young people', *Telegraph*, November 2022.
40. Clement Attlee, 'Great Contemporaries: Lord Attlee on "The Churchill I Knew", Part 1', The Churchill Project, Hillsdale College.
41. Denis Healey, *The Time of My Life*, Michael Joseph, 1989.

6 Discrimination and Disparities

1. Alison Flood, 'Reni Eddo-Lodge becomes first black British author to top UK book charts', *Guardian*, June 2020.
2. Natalie Jerome, 'As a black literary agent, I despair at UK publishing's lack of diversity', *Guardian*, January 2022.
3. NHS workforce by ethnicity, from Gov.UK website.
4. I explored this in my column for the *Observer*: Tomiwa Owolade, 'A rich life in the UK's creative industries is a long shot if you are born poor', *Observer*, December 2022.
5. Sian Bayley, 'Fourth Estate wins 11-way auction for Adegoke's "sensational" debut novel', *The Bookseller*, January 2022.
6. Reni Eddo-Lodge, *Why I'm No Longer Talking to White People About Race*, Bloomsbury, 2018, p.22.
7. Eddo-Lodge, p.34.
8. 'Subnormal: A British Scandal', BBC iPlayer.
9. Haroon Siddique, 'Judiciary in England and Wales institutionally racist, says report', *Guardian*, 18 October 2022.
10. Crest Advisory, 'Forgotten voices: Policing, stop and search and the perspectives of Black children', December 2022.
11. David James Smith, 'Culture of racism, bullying and misogyny revealed in London Fire Brigade', *Sunday Times*, 26 November 2022.
12. GCSE results (Attainment 8), 18 March 2022.

13. FE News, 'Widening participation in higher education', July 2022.
14. Oxford intake by ethnicity, from Facts and Figures page of the University of Oxford website.
15. Permanent exclusions, 24 February 2021.
16. GCSE results (Attainment 8), 18 March 2022.
17. Yohann Koshy, 'We Talked to Akala About Race and Class in the UK', *VICE*, 28 June 2018.
18. Department of Education, Academic Year 2020/21, 'Widening participation in higher education'.
19. Aamna Mohdin, 'Black Caribbean girls in England twice as likely to be excluded from schools as white girls', *Guardian*, 23 September 2021.
20. Catherine Lough, 'Gypsy, Roma and Traveller students "face stark barriers to going to university"', *Evening Standard*, July 2022.
21. Feyisa Demie, 'Raising the achievement of African heritage pupils: A case study of good practice in British schools', *Educational Studies*, December 2007.
22. Chris Millward, 'White students who are left behind: the importance of place', Office for Students, 26 January 2021.
23. Heidi Safia Mirza and Imran Rasul, 'UK ethnic minorities seeing sharp progress in education, but wages and wealth lag behind', Institute for Fiscal Studies, 14 November 2022.
24. KPMG in the UK, 'Social class is the biggest barrier to career progression, KPMG research finds', December 2022.
25. NHS workforce by ethnicity, from Gov.UK website, January 2020.
26. David Lammy, 'Lammy review: final report', 8 September 2017.
27. Stop and search by ethnicity, from Gov.UK website, May 2022.
28. John-Paul Pagano, 'The Loneliest Hatred', *The Tablet*, 28 July 2020.
29. Ben Beaumont-Thomas, 'Wiley posts antisemitic tweets, likening Jews to Ku Klux Klan', *Guardian*, 24 July 2020.
30. Gil Kaufman, 'Ice Cube Criticized For Posting String of Anti-Semitic Images and Conspiracy Theories', *Billboard*, 11 June 2022.
31. Anne Penketh, 'French comedian at centre of Nicolas Anelka row faces ban', *Guardian*, 29 December 2020.
32. The Nation of Islam, *The Secret Relationship Between Blacks and Jews: The Final Call*, 1991.
33. James Hibberd, 'Whoopi Goldberg Apologizes and Seemingly Doubles Down on Holocaust Comments', *Hollywood Reporter*, February 2022.
34. 'Kanye West: Are Jewish fans still listening?', *BBC News*, 6 December 2022.

7 BAME

1. J. B. Priestley, *English Journey*, HarperNorth, 2023, p.35.
2. *We Are Black and British*, BBC Programme, September 2021.
3. Rishi Sunak and Saratha Rajeswaran, *A Portrait of Modern Britain*, Policy Exchange, 6 May 2014.
4. David Cameron, 'We were all white men – so I did something about diversity', *Sunday Times*, July 2022.
5. Trevor Phillips, 'Rishi Sunak's rise is a quiet triumph for British Indians', *The Times*, October 2022.
6. Lola Okolosie, Joseph Harker, Leah Green and Emma Dabiri, 'Is it time to ditch the term black, Asian and minority ethnic (BAME)?', *Guardian*, May 2015.
7. '"Don't call me BAME": Why some people are rejecting the term', *BBC News*, June 2020.
8. Zamila Bunglawala quote from 'Don't call me BAME'.
9. Bonnett, *Multiracism*.
10. Darcus Howe, 'Turning on each other', *Guardian*, August 2004.
11. Jeffrey Boakye, *Black, Listed: Black British Culture Explored*, Dialogue Books, 2019, p.23.
12. Jimi Famurewa, *Settlers: Journeys Through the Food, Faith and Culture of Black African London*, Bloomsbury, 2022, p.25.
13. Famurewa, p.26.
14. Famurewa, p.28.
15. Boakye, *Black, Listed*, p.31.
16. Boakye, p.33.
17. Boakye, p.34.
18. Boakye, p.21.
19. Boakye, p.25.
20. Boakye, p.27.
21. 'Beyoncé – Crazy In Love ft. JAY Z', YouTube.
22. 'Magic System – Premier Gaou', YouTube.
23. Paul Gilroy, *The Black Atlantic: Modernity and Double Consciousness*, Verso, 2022.
24. Sam Moore, 'Wizkid fans despair after O2 show sells out in 12 minutes', *Independent*, 6 August 2021.
25. Boakye, *Black, Listed*, p.155.
26. Boakye, p.202.
27. Boakye, p.207.
28. Boakye, p.210.
29. Du Bois, *The Souls of Black Folk*, p.127.
30. Ralph Wiley quote in Ta-Nehisi Coates, *Between the World and Me*, Text Publishing Company, 2015, p.265.
31. Boakye, *Black, Listed*, p.211.

8 Mixed Race

1. Kwame Anthony Appiah, *The Lies That Bind: Rethinking Identity*, Profile Books, 2019, p.15.
2. Appiah, p.28.
3. Walter White, *A Man Called White: The Autobiography of Walter White*, University of Georgia Press, 1995, p.4.

4. Howard W. French, 'Megalopolis: How coastal west Africa will shape the coming century', *Guardian*, October 2022.
5. Remi Adekoya, *Biracial Britain: What It Means To Be Mixed Race*, Constable, 2021, p.15.
6. Adekoya, p.18.
7. Quote from Chimamanda Ngozi Adichie found in Afua Hirsch, *Brit(ish): On Race, Identity and Belonging*, Jonathan Cape, 2018, p.117.
8. Adekoya, *Biracial Britain*, p.144.
9. Adekoya, p.148.
10. Adekoya, p.184.
11. Barack Obama, *Dreams from My Father: A Story of Race and Inheritance*, Canongate, 2016, p.221.
12. Adekoya, *Biracial Britain*, p.185.
13. Henry Louis Gates, 'Black in Latin America', PBS.
14. Gates, 'Black in Latin America'.
15. Adekoya, *Biracial Britain*, p.190.
16. Gates, 'Black in Latin America'.
17. Afua Hirsch, *Brit(ish): On Race, Identity and Belonging*, Jonathan Cape, 2018, p.22.
18. Hirsch, p.177.
19. Hirsch, p.188.
20. Hirsch, p.30.
21. Hirsch, p.40.
22. Hirsch, p.25.
23. Hirsch, p.168.
24. Bernardine Evaristo, *Manifesto: On Never Giving Up*, Penguin, 2021, p.45.
25. Evaristo, p.30.
26. Evaristo, p.51.
27. Evaristo, p.123.
28. Evaristo, p.128.
29. Kenan Malik, *Not So Black and White: A History of Race from White Supremacy to Identity Politics*, Hurst, 2023, p.65.
30. Appiah, *The Lies That Bind*, p.35.
31. Kwame Anthony Appiah, 'Why are politicians suddenly talking about their 'lived experience?' *Guardian*, November 2020.

9 Black and British

1. Benedict Anderson, *Imagined Communities: Reflections on the Origin and Spread of Nationalism*, Verso, 2006.
2. Jill Lepore, *This America: The Case for the Nation*, John Murray, 2020.
3. Linda Colley, *Britons: Forging the Nation 1707–1837*, Yale University Press, 2009.
4. Jack Lusby, 'Trent Alexander-Arnold shuns the national anthem – and Liverpool fans love it', *This Is Anfield*, June 2022.
5. From Colley, *Britons*, p.145.
6. Daniel Defoe, 'The True Born Englishman'.
7. Colley, *Britons*, p.95.
8. 'Old Firm', Wikipedia.
9. 'Haka', Wikipedia.
10. Ed West, 'England's war with Germany will never be over', *UnHerd*, June 2021.

11. Baddiel, Skinner and Lightning Seeds, 'Three Lions (Football's Coming Home)', YouTube.

12. Harriet Sherwood, 'London more religious than rest of Britain, report finds', *Guardian*, June 2020.

13. '10 Things Bukayo Saka Can't Live Without', *GQ*, April 2022.

14. 'Pizza effect', Wikipedia.

15. Sherwood, 'London more religious than rest of Britain, report finds'.

16. Eric Kaufmann quote from Madeleine Davies, 'Is London more religious now than it was in the days of Margaret Thatcher?', *Church Times*, December 2018.

17. 2021 England and Wales Census.

18. Famurewa, *Settlers*, p.39.

19. Boakye, *Black, Listed*, p.45.

20. Sarah Marsh, 'Alex Mann: the teenage rap fan who lit up Glastonbury', *Guardian*, July 2019.

21. Craig Simpson, 'Wagwan? Street slang to be Britain's main dialect', *Telegraph*, June 2022.

22. Rebecca Mead, 'The Common Tongue of Twenty-First-Century London', *The New Yorker*, 6 February 2022.

23. Michaela Coel, *I May Destroy You*, BBC.

24. Bolu Babalola, 'The Innate Black Britishness of I May Destroy You', *Vulture*, 3 August 2020.

25. Coel, *I May Destroy You*.

26. George Orwell, 'The Lion and the Unicorn: Socialism and the English Genius', The Orwell Foundation.

27. Nesrine Malik, 'I've had to fight: Kehinde Andrews on life as the first UK professor of Black studies', *Guardian*, 4 February 2021.

28. Renie Anjeh, 'Britain's ethnic minority voters are no homogeneous blob', *The Times*, 13 November 2020.

29. 'Attitudes to race and inequality in Great Britain', Ipsos Mori, June 2020.

30. David Starkey, 'The whites have become black', *Newsnight*, YouTube.

31. Caroline Davies, 'Child Q: four Met police officers facing investigation over strip-search', *Guardian*, 15 June 2022.

32. Yinka Bokinni and Zeze Millz, *Unapologetic*, Channel 4.

33. Adrian Wooldridge, 'Britain Needs a Fresh and Frank Approach to Race', *Bloomberg*, January 2023.

ACKNOWLEDGEMENTS

I would like first to thank my agent, Toby Mundy, for encouraging me to write the book. I would also like to thank Mike Harpley for buying the book when he was at Atlantic Books. Very special thanks must go to James Pulford for editing the book and to Mandy Greenfield for her copy-editing. I must also give special thanks to the Royal Society of Literature: winning first prize in the Giles St Aubyn Awards in 2021 greatly supported me in writing the book. Most of the book was written in the London Library, and I would like to thank the staff there. I would also like to thank a group of people who have either read through the book or spoken to me about its contents: Renie Anjeh, Leaf Arbuthnot, Will Lloyd, Will Fear, Charlotte Stroud, Sapan Maini-Thompson and Juliet Samuel. Many thanks to my family: Niyi Owolade, Banke Owolade, Yemi Owolade, Femi Owolade and Yomi Owolade.

INDEX

INDEX

employment, 190–94, 205–7
poverty, 197, 240–41, 259
prejudices between, 231–5
Black History Month, 193
Black Jacobins, The (James), 171
Black Lives Matter protests (2020), 2–5, 113–14, 155, 190, 271–2
UK, impact in, 2–5, 20–21, 174, 177, 179, 229, 290, 295
Black Mass (Gray), 165
Black nationalism, 66–7, 82–3, 95–6, 125, 212, 242
Black Panthers, 12, 90, 95, 219
Black Power movement (1966–1980s), 54
Black Sections movement (1983–93), 153
Black Skin, White Masks (Fanon), 91
Black, Listed (Boakye), 233–6, 240–46
Blackwell's, 189
Bloody Foreigners (Winder), 31
Boakye, Jeffrey, 232, 233–46, 284
Boateng, Paul, 153
Bokinni, Yinka, 297
Bollywood, 231
Bonnett, Alastair, 11
Booker Prize, 263
Bousquet, Ben, 141
Boynton, Robert, 79–80
Brazil, 255
Brexit, 2, 163, 171–3
Bristol, England, 174–8

Brit(ish) (Hirsch), 258
British Book Awards, 189
British Broadcasting Corporation (BBC), 115, 144, 157–8, 178, 215–22, 229, 290
British Empire, 6, 12, 158–85
Brexit and, 171–3
Cyprus, 162
India, 159, 161–2, 165, 172
Ireland, 162
Kenya, 161
Malaya, 162
Nigeria, 167–8
slavery in, 163
British National Party (BNP), 2, 232
British Nationality Act (UK, 1948), 23, 147
British Nationality Act (UK, 1965), 150
British Social Attitudes Survey, 172
Britons (Colley), 276
Brixton, London, 50, 282
Brown v. Board of Education (1954), 100–101
Brown, Elaine, 95–6, 98
Brown, Michael, 3–4
Brown, Noel, 144
Brunel University, 263
Bryan, Anthony, 136–8
Bryanston school, Dorset, 248
Buchanan, Patrick, 74
Buckingham Palace, London, 131, 140
Bunglawala, Zamila, 230
Burna, 239
Bush, Stephen, 172

Butler, Dawn, 179
Butler, Patrick, 197
Butler, Richard Austen 'Rab', 149–50

Cabinet Office, 230
Calhoun, John Caldwell, 69
California, United States, 15
calypso music, 130
Cambridge University, 158, 160, 187, 240, 248, 263, 298
Cameo, 236–7
Cameron, David, 208, 224
Cameroon, 28
Campbell, James, 71
Canada, 147
'cancel culture', 2
Candomblé, 257
'Candy' (Cameo), 236–7
cannabis, 220, 234
capitalism, 96
Capretz, Pierre, 86–9
Caribbean region, 12, 19, 27, 31, 90, 91, 93, 112
Windrush generation, 27, 135–48, 179, 180
Carmichael, Stokely, 53–5, 57, 60, 77, 90, 96, 98
Carty-Williams, Candice, 193
Céline, Louis-Ferdinand, 92
Celtic FC, 277
Celtic people, 28–9, 274
Césaire, Aimé, 59
Channel Four, 231–2, 297
Charlotte, Queen consort, 181–2

INDEX